Jeopardy! champion and New York Times bestselling author

KEN JENNINGS'

JUNIOR GENIUS GUIDES

GREEK MYTHOLOGY

BY **KEN JENNINGS**

ILLUSTRATED BY **MIKE LOWERY**

SEMPER QUAERENS

LITTLE SIMON

New York London Toronto Sydney New Delhi

THE OFFICIAL
JUNIOR GENIUS CIPHER

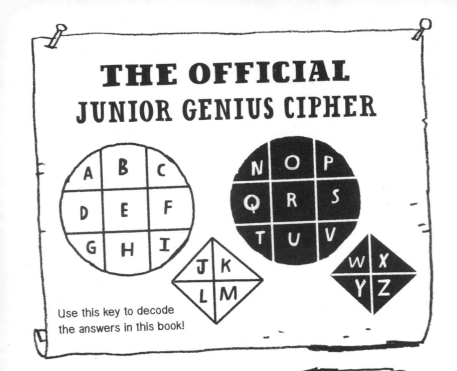

Use this key to decode
the answers in this book!

LITTLE SIMON

An imprint of Simon & Schuster Children's Publishing Division

1230 Avenue of the Americas, New York, New York 10020

Text copyright © 2014 by Ken Jennings

Illustrations copyright © 2014 by Simon & Schuster, Inc.

All rights reserved, including the right of reproduction in whole or in part in any form.

LITTLE SIMON is a registered trademark of Simon & Schuster, Inc., and associated colophon is a trademark of Simon & Schuster, Inc.

For information about special discounts for bulk purchases, please contact Simon & Schuster Special Sales at 1-866-506-1949 or business@simonandschuster.com.

The Simon & Schuster Speakers Bureau can bring authors to your live event. For more information or to book an event contact the Simon & Schuster Speakers Bureau at 1-866-248-3049 or visit our website at www.simonspeakers.com.

Manufactured in China 1113 SCP

First Edition 10 9 8 7 6 5 4 3 2 1

Library of Congress Cataloging-in-Publication Data

Jennings, Ken, 1974- Mythology / by Ken Jennings ; illustrated by Mike Lowery. — First edition.

p. cm. Includes bibliographical references and index. 1. Mythology, Greek—Juvenile literature.

I. Lowery, Mike, 1980- illustrator. II. Title. BL783.J46 2013 398.20938—dc23 2013009833

ISBN 978-1-4424-7330-0 (pbk)

ISBN 978-1-4424-9849-5 (hc)

ISBN 978-1-4424-7331-7 (eBook)

CONTENTS

INTRODUCTION

Good morning, Junior Geniuses! Please take your assigned seats and settle down. Troublemakers in the front row! You know who you are.

My name is Ken Jennings, but you can call me "Professor Jennings" or "Sir" or "Your Grand Sagaciousness." Our subject today is a fascinating one: the classic myths of the Greeks and Romans. That's why I'm wearing this simple white robe, or "toga," even though frankly it's a little chilly, especially when I stand over here by the ventilation panel. Today we will travel back more than three thousand years to the Bronze Age, when these myths were born, in pursuit of one of the only things that really matters in life: knowledge. Lots of knowledge about cool stuff.

The great thing about knowing stuff is that anyone can do it. To be a Junior Genius, all you need to do is pay attention every day to the weird facts in the world around you—and the world is certainly overstuffed with weird facts nowadays. That's why our secret Latin motto is *Semper quaerens*. In English, that just means "Always curious."

Everyone: Stand up, put your right index finger to your temple, and face this drawing of Albert Einstein. We will now say the Junior Genius Pledge.

With all my fellow Junior Geniuses, I solemnly pledge to quest after questions, to angle for answers, to seek out, and to soak up. I will hunger and thirst for knowledge my whole life through, and I dedicate my discoveries to all humankind, with trivia not for just us but for all.

Let's begin!

FIRST PERIOD

Greece Is the Word

Every day we forget stories. I saw a funny video about a cat on the Internet this morning, but when I tried to tell a friend about it, I suddenly had no idea how it ended. A list of best-selling books from ten years ago would have authors on it that I don't even remember. The thing you have to realize about Greek myths is that these are stories so good that we've managed to remember them for more than *three thousand years*.

Three thousand years! When these stories were first told around a banquet table or a campfire, paper hadn't even been invented yet to write them down on. The entire world probably had only forty million people in it—roughly the population of the state of California today. Two of those people were your

GREAT, GREAT
GREAT, GREAT
GREAT,
GREAT, GREAT
GREAT, GREAT
GREAT, GREAT,
GREAT, GREAT,
GREAT, GREAT,
GREAT, GREAT,
GREAT, GREAT,
GREAT, GREAT,
GREAT, GREAT,
GREAT, GREAT,
mm, mm, mm, m
m, mm, mm, m

great-great-great-great- . . . great-grandparents.

Today kids still love Greek myths, but they aren't just fairy tales for children—they've become woven into our everyday life. Have you ever heard anyone say that someone has "the Midas touch" or "an Achilles' heel"? If references like that are all Greek to you, don't worry. It just means that today you're going to hear some great stories for the very first time.

Best of the West

Greek mythology is still important today because so much of Western civilization was born in ancient Greece. Here's a list of some of the things we still use today that the Greeks invented. (Note that some of these inventions cropped up elsewhere—India, China, the Middle East—around the same time.)

○ DEMOCRACY

○ AN ALPHABET with both consonants and vowels (our word "alphabet" even comes from the first two Greek letters, alpha and beta)

Α Β Γ Δ Ε Ζ Η Θ Ι Κ Λ Μ Ν Ξ Ο Π Ρ Σ Τ Υ Φ Χ Ψ Ω

○ LOGIC

○ COMEDY AND DRAMA

○ GEOMETRY

○ WIND POWER

Not too shabby for a handful of small city-states founded by sheep-herders! The Greeks even invented pizza . . . sort of. One of their favorite snacks was an ancestor of pizza called *plakous*: a delicious flatbread sprinkled with herbs, onion, and garlic. (Canadian bacon and pineapple hadn't been invented yet.)

Hero Worship

The greatest Greek inventor was Hero of Alexandria, some-times called Heron. Around AD 40 he invented the world's first steam engine—but, not realizing the machine's potential, only used it as a toy. For Greek temples, Hero invented the world's first automatically opening doors and even a vending machine! (By inserting a coin into a slot, temple visitors could buy a specific amount of holy water.)

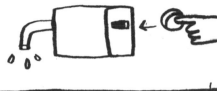

Ancient Greek buildings sometimes had showers and even central heating. Around 600 BC, the Greeks dug a two-thirds mile tunnel on the island of Samos to supply the capital with water. And the Greek explorer Pytheas sailed as far north as Scandinavia!

Greek scientists were not perfect, of course. Even bright guys like Aristotle thought that the Earth was the center of the universe, and that the

AROUND 1960, SCIENTISTS DISCOVERED THAT THIS ANCIENT GREEK DEVICE FOUND IN A SHIP-WRECK WAS ACTUALLY AN EARLY COMPUTER! ASTRONOMERS DESIGNED IT TO CALCULATE POSITIONS OF THE SUN, MOON, AND PLANETS.

heart was the center of human intelligence. (The brain, he said, was just a big cooling organ.) The great Greek mathematician Pythagoras refused to eat (or even touch) beans:

He and his followers were sure that beans had souls!

But in general, the Greeks reached heights of scientific knowledge that wouldn't be surpassed in Europe for almost two thousand years.

Myth Information

But apart from their scientific thinking, the Greeks also had a rich tradition of storytelling about gods and goddesses, brave heroes, and hideous monsters.

What we think of as ancient Greek civilization was actually a big clash of cultures: a series of migrations from the north into the prehistoric civilizations of the Greek isles. Each of these tribes brought their own oral traditions with them, and Greek mythology was what they created from this mishmash of different stories.

The Greeks were polytheists ("pah-lee-THEE-ists"), meaning they believed in many gods. They worshipped these gods by making offerings at stone altars. At home their courtyard would have an altar to a household god. Their village or city would have temples with larger altars

and statues of different gods. Before a family meal, you might sacrifice to Hestia, the goddess of the hearth, with an offering of burned meat. Before beginning a journey, you might travel to a temple of Hermes, the god of travelers, to pray and leave a votive offering (an object like a coin or a small statue) in his sacred grove.

We Found Love

In 1970 a long-lost temple to Aphrodite was unearthed at Knidos, in modern-day Turkey. Aphrodite was the Greek goddess of love, and one of her messengers was the rainbow goddess Iris. Weirdly, the archaeologist who rediscovered the temple was a New York socialite named Iris Love!

When they needed special guidance from the gods, Greeks would go to specific temples and consult oracles. Oracles were priests or (usually) priestesses who spoke on behalf of the gods. At the temple of Apollo at Delphi, the oracle would offer prophecies on the seventh day of every month. She would chew leaves from a sacred laurel tree and inhale volcanic fumes. In a frenzied state, she would then begin to utter strange sounds and words, which priests would translate to visitors.

In myth, the advice from oracles isn't like a weather forecast—it's always 100 percent accurate, no matter what you do to avoid your fate. For example, an oracle once told King Acrisius of Argos that his grandson would kill him one day—and even though he tried to abandon the grandson at sea, the baby survived and grew up to be Perseus, a great hero. Many years later, while Perseus was competing in an athletic contest,  he accidentally threw a discus into the crowd—and killed his grandpa.

King Croesus of Lydia once asked the oracle at Delphi if he should go to war with the Persians. The oracle told him, "If you attack Persia, you will destroy a great empire." Croesus was thrilled and marched his men to war, but lost badly. The empire he destroyed turned out to be his own!

School's Out!

At larger religious feasts and festivals, whole cities would worship the gods together. Athens, the greatest of the ancient Greek mini-kingdoms, had more than one hundred of these festivals every year, so Athenian kids must have had it easy: that's a different holiday every three days or so!

The Greek World

The Greeks believed that Apollo's oracle at Delphi was the center of the world. In one myth Zeus had two birds fly from opposite edges of the world, and a big rock at Delphi called the *omphalos*

marked the exact spot where the birds met. *Omphalos* is Greek for "navel"—they thought of this stone as the earth's belly button! (The earth has an "outie.")

Many Greek scientists, especially in later periods, believed that the earth was round, but in mythology, the earth is a flat disk divided into three continents: Europe, Asia (Asia Minor and the Near East), and Libya (Africa). These lands were surrounded on all sides by Oceanus, the source of all water. Oceanus was a

Titan with six thousand children—can you imagine all the parent-teacher conferences that poor guy had to go to? His three thousand sons were the earth's rivers and his three thousand daughters were ponds and springs.

Mountains were holy places where the gods were known to walk—like Mount Ida, where Zeus was raised, or Mount Helicon, where the Muses sang.

Riding High

The tallest mountain in Greece was Olympus, and because it was often shrouded in clouds, the Greeks believed their gods lived and ruled there. It was said that the mountain was so high that a bronze anvil falling from Olympus to earth would take nine full days and nights to land! (Depending on your math, that means the gods could live as high as 300,000 miles above the world—almost as high as the moon!)

The sky was a dome held up in the west by the Titan Atlas, and many gods traveled across it. The sun was Helios, who kept herds of cattle and sheep—one each for every day of the year—on a faraway island in the east. Every day he drove his fiery chariot across the sky, seeing and hearing everything, like a spy satellite, until he landed in the west at sunset. Then he would sail back home in a great golden cup and feast until dawn.

The moon goddess was Selene, who watched over the earth by night from her silver chariot. Eos, the rosy-fingered goddess of dawn, lived in the east, and the morning dew was her tears after her son Memnon died at Troy.

The Perks of Being a Small Flower

Lots of Greek myths are stories to explain the origin of things in nature, like lightning being the anger of Zeus, or dew being the tears of Eos. Here are three you might not know about.

CLOSE UP

1. THE HYACINTH FLOWER

Hyacinthus was tossing a discus around with the god Apollo when Zephyrus, the mean west wind, blew Apollo's throw off course. Hyacinthus was killed. A bright red hyacinth flower rose from his spilled blood, and the leaves were marked with a pattern like the letters *AI AI*, the sound of Apollo's grief.

2. THE ROOSTER

The gods Ares and Aphrodite asked young Alectryon to warn them when the sun came up, so that Helios wouldn't catch them together. Alectryon fell asleep, so an angry

Ares turned him into a rooster, which is why roosters *always* remember to announce the sunrise.

3. THE MILKY WAY

The hero Heracles was incredibly strong, even as a baby. The first time he was given milk as a newborn, he sucked up so much that he coughed violently, spattering the milk on the heavens, which we can still see today as the Milky Way.

Rolling in the Deep

Beneath the earth was the land of the dead, sometimes called Hades (after the Greek god of the dead) or Erebus. It was a dark and gloomy place. The god Hermes led dead souls there, crossing five rivers:

ACHERON: the river of sorrow
COCYTUS: the river of lamentation
PHLEGETHON: the river of fire
LETHE: the river of forgetfulness
STYX: the river of hate

Greeks would put a coin in a corpse's mouth before it was buried, so that the dead person could use it to pay the ferryman, Charon, to take him across the River Styx.

Three mythical kings—Rhadamanthus, Aeacus, and Minos—would then judge every soul.

Go to Hades! (A Helpful Guide)

ARE YOU BREATHING?

Yes ⇨ STAY OUT!

No ⇦ Welcome to Hades!

DID YOU LIVE A GOOD LIFE?

Yes ⇨ **The Elysian Fields.** A paradise of cool west winds, sports, and music. The soil bears three crops a year, and earth's dead heroes live in peace.

Sometimes ⇦ **The Asphodel Meadows.** A vast, flowered plain, ghostly and boring. No one remembers their name—all memories of life have been wiped away by the River Lethe.

Nope ⇨ **Tartarus.** A pit of terrible winds, surrounded by three layers of night and locked by Poseidon's great bronze doors. It's full of imprisoned monsters as well as mortals who deserved special punishment.

The Buttless Wonder

The hero Theseus sat down on a magic bench in Hades to rest and found himself trapped in the dark for years. Eventually Heracles passed by and managed to pull him up—but Theseus's bottom stayed stuck to the rock! For the rest of his life he was called Theseus Hypolipsos, meaning "rear end rubbed smooth."

When in Rome . . .

Greek mythology got a second lease on life centuries later, when Rome became the world's most powerful empire. The Romans admired the ancient Greeks and borrowed their myths, adapting them to their own gods. Even though the names changed—Zeus became Jupiter, Aphrodite became Venus—the stories stayed the same. (We'll see a full list of the Greek and Roman gods during third period, on page 40.)

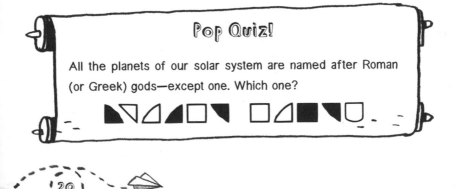

Pop Quiz!

All the planets of our solar system are named after Roman (or Greek) gods—except one. Which one?

The Greek religion didn't survive the spread of Christianity, but its stories have lived on. Our vocabulary has hundreds of words drawn from Greek myth: "hyacinth," from Hyacinthus, whose blood bore the bright red flower, for example, or "ocean" from the waters of Oceanus. You can't even go to the mall without seeing dozens of names and symbols from mythology:

Name	In Mythology	Today
Ajax	a Greek hero of the Trojan War	a cleaning powder
Amazon	a tribe of warrior women	an online retailer
Mercury	the Roman name for Hermes	a car
Midas	a king with a "golden touch"	a muffler shop
Nike	the goddess of victory	a shoe
Olympus	the mountain of the gods	a camera
Pandora	the first woman	an Internet radio service

Even three thousand years later, if you don't know these stories, you're really myth-ing out.

SECOND PERIOD

In the Beginning

World mythologies almost always have a creation myth explaining how the world came to be. Greek mythology is woven from three different kinds of stories: some told by prehistoric natives of Greece, some brought by invasions from the north, and some borrowed from the ancient myths of Asia Minor. Some of these people worshipped peaceful earth goddesses; others worshipped mighty sky gods. That's why the Greek creation story begins with an earth goddess and ends with a sky god.

Mother Earth

Gaea ("JEE-uh"), the earth, was first born out of the darkness of Chaos. She was empty and desolate as she slept. Uranus, the sky, looked down at her from above

and fell in love. When the sky rained on the earth, lakes and seas appeared. Gaea's soil became fertile, and plants began to grow.

A Family Affair

In most versions of the story, Gaea gives birth first to Uranus, which means she's in a relationship *with her own son*. I know it's yucky, but you're going to have to get used to this sort of thing in Greek mythology. Gods be marrying their sisters and people be marrying their parents *all the time*.

Not all the children were such a success, though. Gaea's first humanoid children were triplets: hundred-handed giants named Briareus, Cottus, and Gyges. The next birth was triplets as well: wild, one-eyed Cyclopes named

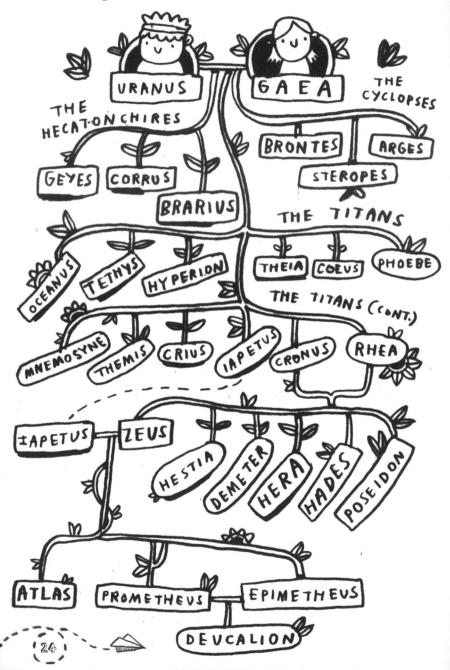

Brontes, Steropes, and Arges. To the Greeks, these giants all represented powerful forces of nature: lightning and thunder and earthquakes. Uranus was unhappy to have noisy monsters as children, and threw them into the pit of Tartarus. Some dad!

Mothers love even their ugly children, of course, and Gaea was furious. Her next children were the Titans, twelve powerful deities led by the youngest of them, Cronus. Gaea gave Cronus a stone sickle and persuaded

him to attack Uranus. Cronus mutilated his father with the great sickle. Uranus's blood rained down on the earth, which then gave birth to new creatures like nymphs and the three terrible Furies. Cronus was now the ruler of the universe.

The Hard Stuff

Cronus's sickle was made of adamant, a mythical rock that sometimes shows up in Greek myth. (The Titan Prometheus is later chained to a mountain with adamantine bonds.) Adamant might represent flint or diamond or something ever stronger—the point is that it's really, *really* unbreakably hard.

Clash of the Titans

Don't get too used to Cronus, Junior Geniuses! What goes around, comes around.

His parents had prophesied that just as Cronus had overthrown his father, he would be overthrown by his own son. So when he and his wife, the Titaness Rhea, had children of their own, Cronus did what any father would do under these circumstances: He ate them.

That's right, he ate the newborn babies. Little Hestia, Demeter, Hera, Hades, and Poseidon went right into his belly. Suddenly Uranus's parenting isn't looking so bad, right?

World's Greatest Dads

Uranus and Cronus aren't the best fathers in Greek mythology, but they have plenty of company. Here are stories of some other lousy dads, with their parenting skills ranked from 1 (least terrible) to 5 (most terrible) "World's Greatest Dad" mugs:

AGAMEMNON Sacrificed his daughter Iphigenia to the goddess Artemis so that the wind would change and his fleet could sail to Troy.

ACRISIUS Afraid of a prophecy that his grandson would kill him, he locked his daughter Danae in a bronze cell to keep her childless.

SCHOENENUS Made his daughter Atalanta agree to marry the first man who could beat her in a footrace.

LAIUS Abandoned his baby son Oedipus on a remote mountain with the newborn's feet staked to the ground.

Rhea was understandably annoyed at this turn of events, so when she was pregnant with a third son, she hatched a plan.

MY PLAN by Rhea

1. Sneak away and give birth in the dead of night on a mountain in Arcadia so secret that nobody even casts a shadow there.

2. Leave my baby to be raised there by nymphs and the goat Amaltheia.

3. Station my servants, the Curetes, next to the baby's golden cradle, banging on spears and shields to drown out his crying, so Cronus won't hear.

4. Wrap a baby-size rock in swaddling clothes and feed it to MY DEAR HUSBAND.

The plan went perfectly! Zeus was raised by Amaltheia on Mount Ida, and when she died, he placed her in the heavens as the constellation Capricorn. He gave one of her horns to the nymphs who had cared for him, and it would bring forth food and drink whenever called upon. This is where our symbol of the "horn of plenty" comes from.

Pop Quiz!

What ten-letter Latin word, literally meaning "horn of plenty," do we sometimes use for this symbol?

When Zeus was old enough, he and Rhea prepared a potion that would make Cronus sick, and she slipped it into her husband's drink. He got so violently ill that he barfed up all five of his swallowed children! Still angry at the whole swallowing-them-for-years-and-then-barfing-them-up thing, they decided to overthrow their father.

For ten years a terrible war raged among the gods. Cronus and the other Titans chose Iapetus's son, the mighty Atlas, as their commander. Zeus released the Cyclopes and the hundred-handed giants (or Hecatonchires) from Tartarus. The forests burned and the sea boiled as the giants threw three hundred boulders at a time (one with each hand!) down at their enemies below, like a battery of heavy machine guns.

The war finally ended when the Cyclopes, master smiths, forged three amazing weapons for Zeus and his brothers:

ZEUS   POSEIDON   HADES

These three gods orchestrated a commando raid on the Titans' HQ on Mount Othrys. Under cover of invisibility from Hades's helmet the three sneaked in, and Poseidon distracted Cronus with his trident while Zeus struck him down with a thunderbolt. The Titans were banished, and their leader, Atlas, was given the special punishment of holding up the sky. (Why didn't the sky ever fall down *before* Atlas was on the job? Mythology does not reveal this.)

Pop Quiz!

Because his name sounds like "Chronos," Cronus was later identified with a mythical figure we still see today—and one who still holds a harvesting sickle or scythe. What is Cronus's modern-day alter ego?

Locked Out of Heaven

Notice who hasn't been created yet: Us! People!

Atlas's brothers Prometheus and Epimetheus were Titans who fought on Zeus's side. They formed the first people out of clay—in Panopeus, a city where, the Greeks said, the clay still smelled like human skin. (Eww.)

Epimetheus created all the animals. Prometheus sculpted man standing upright and looking toward heaven, more like the gods than like the other beasts. Epimetheus had already given the best gifts (great strength or speed or warm coats) to the animals, so Prometheus taught humans important skills instead: to build houses, herd cattle, read and write, understand the seasons and stars, and so on.

The gods were already getting pretty fed up with Prometheus when he made his fatal mistake. In teaching men to offer sacrifices to the gods, he played a trick. He divided a bull into two parts.

GROSS ORGANS AND STUFF

RICH WHITE FAT

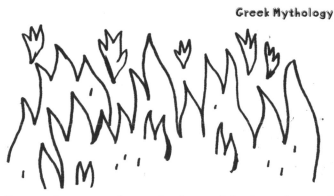

Zeus, of course, chose the beautiful white fat, and was *furious* when he found out about the switcheroo. "Let them eat their meat raw, then!" he said, withholding the gift of fire.

So Prometheus stole into Olympus and hid a spark of fire from the sun's chariot inside the hollow stalk of a fennel plant. He brought fire down to earth so that the poor shivering men could heat their homes and cook their meals.

The gods had their revenge. First Zeus ordered Prometheus chained to a mountain pillar. Every day a vulture would fly in and devour his liver, which

would grow back every night. Prometheus would endure this torture forever.

His brother had it even worse. Epimetheus's punishment was . . . marriage.

Thinking Outside the Box

Hephaestus, the Greek god of the forge, sculpted the first woman out of clay, and many of his fellow gods gave her gifts.

- THE FOUR WINDS: the breath of life

- APHRODITE: grace and beauty

- ATHENA: skill in weaving

- HERMES: speech and a knack for trickery

- THE GRACES: fine jewelry

- THE HOURS: a crown of flowers

- ZEUS: curiosity

They named her Pandora, meaning "all gifts." She became Epimetheus's wife, but she brought with her one other gift: a jar she had been instructed never to open.

When Is a Box Not a Box

Yup, Pandora had a *pithos*, a big pottery jar used to carry liquids and grains. In the sixteenth century, a Dutch writer named Erasmus mistranslated *pithos* into Latin as *pyxis*, or "box." Ever since, we've mistakenly believed Pandora owned a box.

Eventually Pandora's insatiable curiosity got the better of her and she peeked into the jar. Out flew all the evils that have tormented humanity ever since: Sickness, Old Age, Sin, Madness, Drudgery, and all the rest. Luckily, Pandora closed the jar before its last occupant, Hope, could escape.

Survivor: Greece!

Prometheus's son Deucalion was warned by his imprisoned father that an angry Zeus was planning to destroy the human race for its many sins. So Deucalion and his wife, Pyrrha, built a large chest, or ark, on which to ride out the coming flood. (Like most ancient cultures, including the Hebrews, the Greeks believed in a primeval Great Flood caused by an angry god.)

Deucalion and Pyrrha floated for nine days before the waters subsided and their ark came to rest on a mountain. Then they offered a sacrifice to Zeus from a temple still dripping with water and seaweed, and the gods told them, "Throw the bones of your mother behind you!"

This was confusing advice! Deucalion finally decided that the "mother" in the prophecy referred to the earth, Gaea, and her bones were the rocks. They threw rocks behind their heads, and wherever the rocks landed, men and women appeared to repopulate the earth. This is why the words for "pebble" and "people" are similar. (In Greek, the pun is on the words *laas*, or stone, and *laos*, or people.)

Luckily, it's not as rainy today as it was back in Deucalion's day. Line up by the playground door for recess, Junior Geniuses!

RECESS

Junior Geniuses, if you like sports, you owe a lot to the ancient Greeks. Our modern Olympics started with a Greek tradition: holding a big athletic contest every four years outside the temples at Olympia. In one myth, the first Olympic games were a series of races held to entertain the newborn baby Zeus while he was hiding from his father, Cronus.

The athletes at the ancient Olympics usually competed naked! Please don't try that at recess, but here are some other Greek-flavored games you might like:

Pentathlon

Today's modern Olympic decathlon comes from the ancient five-sport Greek pentathlon, which included the long jump, discus throw, javelin throw, sprinting, and wrestling. Organize your own outdoor pentathlon, using a Frisbee for the discus throw, a stick for the javelin, and thumb-wrestling instead of real wrestling. Award homemade medals to the top three finishers in each event.

Medusa Tag

Just like freeze tag, except that the tagging player is "Medusa" rather than "it." (Bonus points if "it" wears snakes in his or her hair!) Once you've been tagged, you're a stone statue until another player heals you with the Rod of Asclepius, the Greek god of medicine. (In other words, by tapping you with a stick.)

Pandora's Box

Pandora's box (well, jar) contained all the evils of the world. On small slips  of paper, you and a group of friends each write the name of five well-known people or things you dislike: "cantaloupe," "homework," "Jar Jar Binks," and so on. (The  game works best with a large group of players: six to eight or even more.) Fold each paper in half and place it in a small container, like a jar or bowl.

Now divide into two teams. One player from each team pulls out slips of paper one at a time and gives verbal clues to his or her teammates until they guess the word or name on the paper. Keep track of how many of the world's evils your team guesses in one minute, and then let the other team have a turn.

There's one twist: an additional folded piece of paper in the container has the word "hope" on it. The game ends as soon as "hope" escapes from Pandora's box, and the team that's guessed the most words at that time is the winner!

THIRD PERIOD

The Gods of Olympus

After the Titans were defeated, Zeus and his five brothers and sisters began their reign over all of creation. The Cyclopes who had helped them win the war now used their skills of craftsmanship to build the gods a new home: a glittering palace atop Mount Olympus.

Did Anyone Ever Try to Climb Mount Olympus?

The highest point in modern Greece is still Mount Olympus, a 7,700-foot peak in northern Thessaly. Readers of Greek mythology will often wonder: Did the Greeks ever climb up there and find out if the stories about their gods were actually true?

In fact, Mount Olympus is not a tough hike, and over ten thousand people still make it to the top every year. Some get up and down in a single day! The ancient Greeks could see its peak in clear weather, and could easily tell that there was no magical palace on top.

But the Olympus in Greek stories isn't really a single geographical mountain. Sometimes it was clearly noted to be the Olympus in Thessaly, yes—but in other stories it was identified with other mountains elsewhere. In later tellings, the gods' home is a palace hidden somewhere in the sky, and not on a real mountaintop at all.

Even though the Greeks imagined their gods to have almost indescribable power, they certainly weren't perfect.

LIKE MORTALS . . .

○ The gods lived together as a big family: parents, spouses, children, etc.

○ They each had their own jobs and specialties. Zeus and his brothers drew lots, and that's how Zeus became god of the sky, Poseidon god of the sea, and Hades god of the underworld.

○ They enjoyed feasting, drinking, gossip, and other human pastimes.

○ They had human emotions: anger, desire, jealousy, etc.

○ Their actions were sometimes admirable, but sometimes definitely not.

○ They could be physically hurt or wounded.

UNLIKE MORTALS . . .

○ The gods were physically huge! When Ares fell at Troy, Homer said his body stretched seven hundred feet.

○ They were beautiful and literally glowed. Instead of blood, a golden substance called ichor ("EYE-core") ran through their veins.

○ They enjoyed the aroma of burned offerings but ate and drank only ambrosia and nectar.

○ This food, brought to Zeus by doves from somewhere far out to sea in the west, made them immortal.

○ They had a wide variety of superpowers, including strength, speed, keen perception, knowledge of the future, and the ability to change shape.

Smooth Operator

Zeus chose his older sister Hera to be his queen and rule at his side. As with many mortal men, this took some persuasion and even a little trickery. When Hera refused his offer of marriage, Zeus disguised himself as a little cuckoo and created a great thunderstorm. Hera saw the bedraggled bird struggling through the storm and held it close to keep the poor thing dry. That's when Zeus turned back into his godly self.

Unfortunately, Zeus kept up this kind of trickery even once he and Hera were married. He was a chronic womanizer, always falling for some new pretty face—mortal or immortal, he didn't care. A new generation of Olympian gods was born from Zeus's *many* relationships.

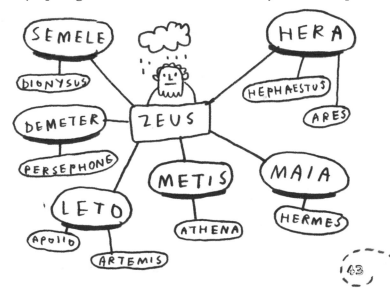

My Dad Can Beat Up Your Dad!

The reason why the gods were said to have so many love affairs with mortal women was so that lots of kings and other ancient bigwigs could claim divine descent. "Of course I'm king! Zeus was my great-grandpa!"

These younger gods joined Zeus and his siblings in the majestic throne room of Olympus, where they ruled together over the earth below.

Born This Way

Many of the Olympian gods had a slightly weird birth. Here are some highlights:

APHRODITE emerged fully grown from sea foam at the spot where Uranus's mutilated body parts had been cast down into the sea.

APOLLO'S pregnant mother, Leto, wandered the earth, as a jealous Hera had ordered all the lands of the world not to admit her. Finally, she found sanctuary on the floating island

APHRODITE

of Delos and hid beneath a palm tree to give birth. Even then, Hera forbade the goddess of childbirth, Eileithyia, from attending her, so the labor pains stretched on and on. Finally the gods distracted Hera with a beautiful necklace, Eileithyia escaped to Delos, and Apollo was born.

ARTEMIS helped her mother, Leto, deliver her twin brother, Apollo. She was just nine days old. Kids grew up so fast those days!

ARES doesn't even have a father in some stories! Hera becomes pregnant after a flower goddess has her touch a mysterious, magical bloom.

ATHENA's birth was a real headache. Afraid that their child would depose him, Zeus swallowed the pregnant Metis, the goddess of prudence. This made him wiser, but soon he started having terrible throbbing headaches. Hephaestus pried open Zeus's skull, and out jumped Athena, fully grown and armed.

ATHENA

HEPHAESTUS was so sickly at birth that Hera, disgusted, threw him from heaven. He fell an entire day before he landed with a huge boom, causing an earthquake on the isle of Lemnos. Hephaestus was left crippled by the fall, and from then on he put the "limp" back in "Olympus."

HERMES wandered out of his mother's cave on the day he was born and stole all of Apollo's cattle! Here's what he did: He made special shoes out of tree bark for the cows, so, as he led them back to his cave, it looked like their tracks were headed the other way. He was already back in his cradle pretending to nap when Apollo finally figured out the trick. Hermes had also spent part of his busy morning inventing the lyre out of a tortoiseshell, so he and Apollo cut a deal: Hermes could keep the cows, but Apollo got the first lyre.

ZEUS was raised by a goat-nymph, while his dad swallowed a rock thinking it was him.

The Big 12

Because the Greeks considered twelve to be a particularly beautiful number, their descriptions of their pantheon

(set of gods) always included twelve Olympian gods. Unfortunately the math doesn't quite work out.

There are fourteen gods for just twelve spots!

Different writers solved this problem in different ways. Hades was often dropped from the list because his throne was deep beneath the earth in the land of the dead, not on high Olympus. Sometimes Dionysus was dropped as well because, unlike all the other Olympian gods, he was only half-divine: His mother was a mortal woman.

In the most common version, Hestia, the goddess of the home, volunteers to give up her spot so that Dionysus can join the pantheon. Instead of a throne, she humbly chooses to tend the hearth of Olympus. This solution makes sense, as Hestia was an important goddess in the Greeks' daily worship, but there were hardly any myths about her at all.

If the Greek gods had their own set of trading cards, it would probably look something like this. Collect all twelve! Er, fourteen.

GREEK GODS TRADING CARDS!

Zeus

("zooss")

Symbols

eagle

oak

bull

God of: the sky, thunder, law, justice

Roman names: Jupiter, Jove
Other titles: "cloud-gatherer," "thunderer," "far-seeing"
Parents: Cronus and Rhea ∘ **Spouse:** Hera
Children: Apollo, Ares, Artemis, Athena, Dionysus, the Fates, the Graces, Helen of Troy, Heracles, Hermes, the Muses, Persephone, Perseus, dozens of others
Personality: strong leader, hopeless womanizer
Powers & skills: strength, wisdom (from swallowing Metis, goddess of prudence!), control of the weather, ability to turn mortals immortal
Wears or wields: thunderbolts, a scepter
Attendants: Hebe and later Ganymede (cupbearer), Cyclopes (forge thunderbolts), Pegasus (carries thunderbolts), Nike, Kratos, Bia, and Zelus (gods of victory, power, force, and zeal)
Special sacrifice: any white animal on a raised altar
Chariot pulled by: the four winds (in the shape of horses)
BONUS FACT! According to Homer, Zeus was so strong that he could challenge all the other Olympian gods to a tug-of-war using a golden chain—and win single-handedly.

Hera

("HEH-ruh")

Symbols

lily

cow

cuckoo

Goddess of: marriage, women, childbirth

Roman name: Juno
Other titles: "white-armed," "cow-eyed"
Parents: Cronus and Rhea
Spouse: Zeus
Children: Ares, Eileithyia, Eris, Hebe, Hephaestus
Personality: queenly, jealous
Wears or wields: a crown and a lotus-scepter
Attendants: Eileithyia (goddess of childbirth), Hebe (goddess of youth), Iris (the rainbow goddess), Hesperides (who guards her orchard), the Hours
Special sacrifice: goats
Chariot pulled by: peacocks

BONUS FACT! Hera once plotted to overthrow Zeus, binding him to his bed with one hundred rawhide knots. When Zeus got free, he took revenge by hanging Hera from the sky with anvils chained to her feet. Ouch.

Poseidon

("puh-SYE-dun")

Symbols

dolphin

horse

seashell

God of: the sea, earthquakes, horses

Roman name: Neptune
Other titles: "earth-shaker," "dark-haired one," "tamer of horses"
Parents: Cronus and Rhea
Spouse: Amphitrite
Children: Orion, Polyphemus, Theseus, Triton
Personality: changeable as the sea—sometimes calm,
but quick to anger
Powers & Skills: control of the sea, to raise storms or
ensure calm passage
Wears or wields: a trident
Attendants: Proteus and Nereus (sea gods), nereids (sea nymphs)
Special sacrifice: horses—at sea, drowned horses
Chariot pulled by: Hippocamps (half horse, half fish)
BONUS FACT! In the *Iliad*, Poseidon travels from Olympus to
his undersea palace in just three mighty strides, which made the
mountains themselves tremble!

Hades

("HAY-deez")

Symbols

cypress

narcissus

horn of wealth

God of: the underworld, the dead, wealth

Roman names: Dis, Orcus, Pluto
Other titles: "the rich one"
Parents: Cronus and Rhea
Spouse: Persephone
Children: Zagreus, Melinoe, Macaria
Personality: grim, merciless
Powers & skills: control over the spirits of the dead, invisibility
Wears or wields: a helmet of invisibility, a two-pronged pitchfork, the keys to the underworld
Attendants: the Furies, Hecate (goddess of magic), Cerberus (three-headed dog)
Special sacrifice: black rams and ewes, with the blood allowed to drain into the earth
Chariot pulled by: black horses
BONUS FACT! The Greeks were so frightened of Hades that they turned their heads away while sacrificing to him and wouldn't even utter his name, instead calling him "Plouton," the rich one, since he possessed all the earth's underground mineral wealth.

Demeter

("di-MEE-tur")

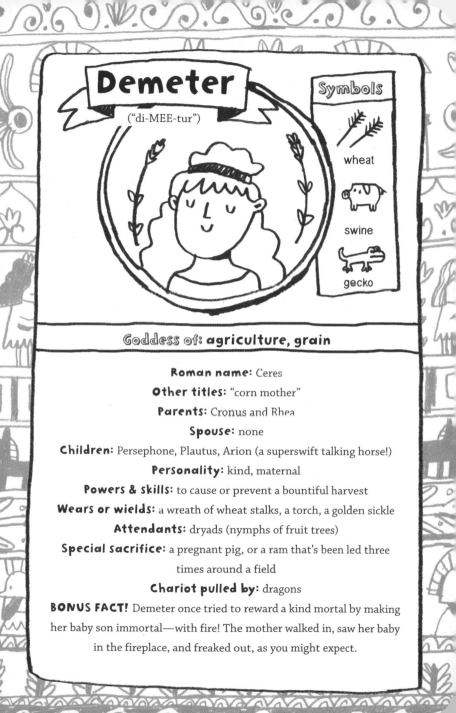

Symbols

wheat

swine

gecko

Goddess of: agriculture, grain

Roman name: Ceres

Other titles: "corn mother"

Parents: Cronus and Rhea

Spouse: none

Children: Persephone, Plautus, Arion (a superswift talking horse!)

Personality: kind, maternal

Powers & skills: to cause or prevent a bountiful harvest

Wears or wields: a wreath of wheat stalks, a torch, a golden sickle

Attendants: dryads (nymphs of fruit trees)

Special sacrifice: a pregnant pig, or a ram that's been led three times around a field

Chariot pulled by: dragons

BONUS FACT! Demeter once tried to reward a kind mortal by making her baby son immortal—with fire! The mother walked in, saw her baby in the fireplace, and freaked out, as you might expect.

Hestia

("HESS-tee-uh")

Symbols

flame

kettle

Goddess of: **home, hearth**

Roman name: Vesta

Other titles: "the eldest"

Parents: Cronus and Rhea

Spouse: Nope—maiden goddess

Children: none

Personality: gentle, modest

Wears or wields: a veil over her head, a flowering branch

Special sacrifice: a domestic pig, as well as the first offering from *every* household sacrifice

BONUS FACT! Hestia was both the oldest *and* the youngest of Zeus's siblings! She was the firstborn to Rhea, but the last to be vomited up by her father Cronus.

Aphrodite

("aff-ruh-DYE-tee")

Symbols
- swan
- apple
- rabbit

Goddess of: love, beauty, pleasure

Roman name: Venus
Other titles: "laughter-loving," "foam-born," "golden"
Parents: Uranus, sort of • **Spouse:** Hephaestus
Children: Eros, Harmonia, Aeneas
Personality: joyful, flirtatious
Powers & skills: could create feelings of desire in both gods and mortals
Wears or wields: her cestus, a magic girdle that could make anyone fall in love with her
Attendants: Eros, Himeros, Pothos (gods of love), the Graces
Special sacrifice: anything but a pig, since a boar killed her beloved Adonis ("sacrificing swine to Aphrodite" was an old Greek proverb for giving someone a lame gift)
Chariot pulled by: sparrows
BONUS FACT! The sculptor Praxiteles once carved a statue of Aphrodite so beautiful that the island of Kos was scandalized and rejected it! It wound up in Aphrodite's temple at Knidos, where visiting young men would often fall in love with it.

Apollo

("uh-PAH-loh")

Symbols

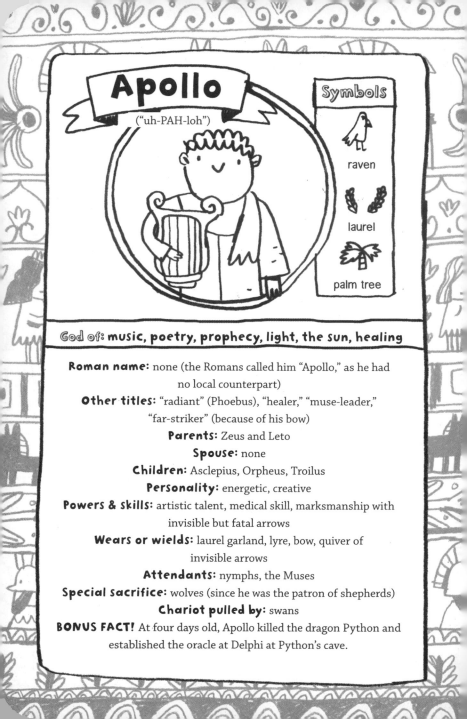

raven

laurel

palm tree

God of: music, poetry, prophecy, light, the sun, healing

Roman name: none (the Romans called him "Apollo," as he had no local counterpart)

Other titles: "radiant" (Phoebus), "healer," "muse-leader," "far-striker" (because of his bow)

Parents: Zeus and Leto

Spouse: none

Children: Asclepius, Orpheus, Troilus

Personality: energetic, creative

Powers & skills: artistic talent, medical skill, marksmanship with invisible but fatal arrows

Wears or wields: laurel garland, lyre, bow, quiver of invisible arrows

Attendants: nymphs, the Muses

Special sacrifice: wolves (since he was the patron of shepherds)

Chariot pulled by: swans

BONUS FACT! At four days old, Apollo killed the dragon Python and established the oracle at Delphi at Python's cave.

Artemis
("ART-uh-miss")

Symbols

hound

walnut

quail

Goddess of: the hunt, the wilderness, the moon

Roman name: Diana
Other titles: "huntress," "showerer of arrows," "mistress of animals," "light bringer"
Parents: Zeus and Leto
Spouse: nope—maiden goddess
Children: none
Personality: proud, fierce
Powers & skills: invented hunting, amazing aim with her invisible but fatal arrows
Wears or wields: hunting tunic, golden bow and quiver
Attendants: Orion (her only male hunting companion); Arethusa, Callisto and other nymphs
Special sacrifice: in some places, human sacrifice!
Chariot pulled by: four silver stags with golden antlers
BONUS FACT! Zeus doted on Artemis and granted her six wishes as a young girl. She used some of the wishes well—asking for all the mountains as her realm, for example—but others not so well. She wasted one asking for a nice knee-length tunic!

Athena

("uh-THEE-nuh")

Symbols

owl

serpent

rooster

Goddess of: wisdom, courage, crafts, heroism

Roman name: Minerva

Other titles: Pallas, "gray-eyed," "horsewoman," "head-born," "guardian of the city"

Parents: Zeus and Metis

Spouse: nope—maiden goddess

Children: none

Personality: brave, creative, proud

Powers & skills: invented weaving, shipbuilding, pottery, many other crafts

Wears or wields: helmet, armor, spear, the aegis (a shield of goatskin with Medusa's head mounted on it)

Attendants: Nike (goddess of victory)

Special sacrifice: bulls—but not goats, due to her aegis

Chariot pulled by: horses—and it was the first chariot, since she invented it!

BONUS FACT! Medusa used to be a beautiful young priestess of Athena, before Athena caught her breaking her vows and made her as ugly as her sister Gorgons.

Ares

("EH-reez")

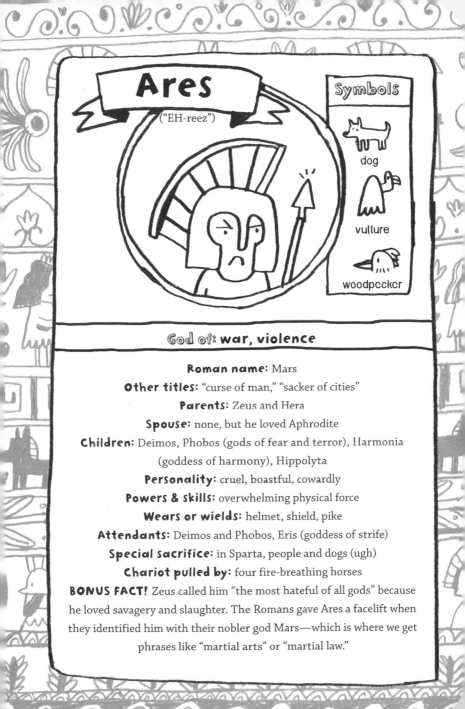

Symbols

dog

vulture

woodpecker

God of: war, violence

Roman name: Mars
Other titles: "curse of man," "sacker of cities"
Parents: Zeus and Hera
Spouse: none, but he loved Aphrodite
Children: Deimos, Phobos (gods of fear and terror), Harmonia
(goddess of harmony), Hippolyta
Personality: cruel, boastful, cowardly
Powers & skills: overwhelming physical force
Wears or wields: helmet, shield, pike
Attendants: Deimos and Phobos, Eris (goddess of strife)
Special sacrifice: in Sparta, people and dogs (ugh)
Chariot pulled by: four fire-breathing horses
BONUS FACT! Zeus called him "the most hateful of all gods" because
he loved savagery and slaughter. The Romans gave Ares a facelift when
they identified him with their nobler god Mars—which is where we get
phrases like "martial arts" or "martial law."

Hephaestus

("hif-FESS-tus")

Symbols

anvil

donkey

crane

God of: fire, blacksmiths, volcanoes

Roman names: Vulcan, Mulciber
Other titles: "the lame one," "skillful"
Parents: Zeus and Hera
Spouse: Aphrodite
Children: King Erichthonius of Athens
Personality: kind, hardworking
Powers & skills: an amazing talent for metalworking, masonry, sculpture, and other crafts
Wears or wields: hammer, tongs, workman's cap
Attendants: Cyclopes, golden mechanical servants
Special sacrifice: animal fat burned over his special flame
Chariot pulled by: instead of a chariot, he rode a donkey or a rolling mechanical throne

BONUS FACT! When the gods took King Laomedon's son Ganymede to be their new cupbearer, Hephaestus made the king a consolation prize: a magical grapevine of gold.

Hermes

("HUR-meez")

Symbols

tortoise

ram

hawk

God of: trade, travelers, shepherds, thieves

Roman name: Mercury

Other titles: "Argus slayer," "messenger"

Parents: Zeus and Maia

Spouse: none

Children: Pan (the god of goatherds), Hermaphroditus

Personality: clever, mischievous, helpful

Powers & skills: the speed of the wind, ability to conduct the dead to the underworld, quick wits, a persuasive tongue, the ability to put people to sleep with his wand

Wears or wields: winged sandals, a winged traveler's hat, caduceus (a rod with serpents wrapped around it), a golden blade

Attendants: Pan and his satyrs, the oreads (mountain nymphs)

Special sacrifice: lambs and young goats

BONUS FACT! The Greek equivalent of highway signs were roadside piles of stones called *hermai*, associated with the god of travelers.

Dionysus

("dye-uh-NYE-suss")

Symbols

grapevine

bull

wild donkey

God of: **wine, merrymaking**

Roman names: Bacchus and Liber
Other titles: "twice-born," "the mad one"
Parents: Zeus and Semele
Spouse: Ariadne
Children: Priapus (god of fertility), Deianeira (wife of Heracles)
Personality: rowdy, fun-loving
Powers & skills: winemaking, beekeeping, ability to drive mortals mad
Wears or wields: crown of ivy, thyrsus (a staff tipped with a pine cone), cantharus (wine cup) that magically refilled itself
Attendants: Pan, Silenus (god of drunkenness), maenads (frenzied revelers), satyrs, centaurs, and all kinds of other party animals
Chariot pulled by: leopards
Special sacrifice: a goat, torn apart the way grapevines are at harvest
BONUS FACT! Dionysus's cult got so crazy that, for a time, in Rome it was made illegal to worship him.

Feud of the Gods

Typically the Greek gods got along pretty well. But they're essentially a family, and like any family, they had their little squabbles. Even Zeus and Hera didn't always get along, after all. Here are five family feuds that sometimes made life on Olympus a little tense.

Apollo's son Asclepius was such a brilliant healer that he could even resurrect the dead. Hades worried that the underworld would start to get lonely if all the dead left, and complained to Zeus, so Zeus struck down Asclepius with a thunderbolt. Apollo was furious and killed the Cyclopes in revenge. An angry Zeus banished Apollo from Olympus for a year of hard labor herding sheep and shoveling poop for King Admetus of Therae.

Athena vs. Poseidon

Athena and Poseidon both claimed the Greek land of Attica, so they decided to hold a contest of gifts, with the city there as the prize. Poseidon offered the first gift:

He struck the hillside with this trident and a mighty spring of water burst forth, to the amazement of the people. But Poseidon was a sea god, and so the spring was seawater, too salty to be drinkable. Athena, in her turn, planted the first olive tree, which provided food, oil, wood, and shade. The people chose Athena to be their patron, and that's how the city got its name: Athens.

Hades vs. Demeter

Hades wanted a queen, but what nice girl wants to live in the underworld? Desperate, Hades asked Zeus for the hand of Demeter's lovely daughter Persephone ("pur-SEFF-uh-nee"). Zeus waffled on the idea, so Hades decided he should just kidnap Persephone. One day while she was picking wildflowers in a meadow, the ground cracked open and Hades emerged, pulling Persephone down into the earth in his black chariot. Demeter, heartbroken, wandered the world for nine days and nights looking for her daughter. Plants withered and the earth became barren. Finally, she found a swineherd who had

seen the abduction and (as they say on cop shows) could ID Hades as the "perp." Demeter threatened Zeus that no crops would ever grow again unless he returned her daughter. Zeus agreed to Demeter's demand—as long as Persephone hadn't eaten the food of the dead. But Persephone had been tricked: She'd tasted three seeds of a pomegranate in Hades's realm. As a result, Zeus decreed that Persephone should spend three months of every year under the earth, and the other nine months in the sunlight with her mother. This is why, said the Greeks, the earth grows cold and plants die three months out of every year—Demeter is mourning.

Ares {VS.} **Hephaestus**

Zeus gave the beautiful Aphrodite in marriage to Hephaestus, who doted on her. But as the goddess of love, she wasn't content with just one man. When Helios, the sun, reported to Hephaestus that he'd seen Aphrodite with Ares, the handsome god of war (see page 17), Hephaestus, fuming, went back to his forge and hammered out an amazing unbreakable bronze net, then planted it as a booby trap to catch Ares and Aphrodite in their next meeting together. When the trap was sprung, Hephaestus gathered all the gods around to laugh at Ares's humiliation. Hephaestus couldn't bring himself to divorce Aphrodite, but he did demand that Ares pay him the complete price of every gift he and Aphrodite had received on their wedding day.

Zeus had a wandering eye as well, of course, and Hera tried to keep him in line by going ninety-nine eyes better! She had a hundred-eyed servant named Argus keep watch over Zeus at all times. This cramped Zeus's style, so he sent Hermes to take care of the problem. Hermes played lullabies on his flute until Argus's eyes all closed in sleep, and then Hermes killed the watchman with a boulder. Hera was terribly angry with Hermes and

placed Argus's hundred eyes in the tail of her own favorite animal, the peacock. This is why peacocks have bright eye-shapes in their tail feathers today.

Pop Quiz!

One of the mortal women Zeus romanced was a Phoenician princess he carried to Crete on his back—and today a whole continent is named for her. What was her name?

⬜ ◼ ◼ ◼ ◣ ◿

ART CLASS

When you look at the night sky, do you see shapes in the patterns of the stars? These patterns are called constellations, and most of our eighty-eight modern constellations are the exact same ones imagined by the Greeks and Romans thousands of years ago.

In Greek mythology, Zeus would often immortalize a fallen hero or creature by placing its shape in the stars. You've probably seen the Big Dipper? It's actually part of a constellation called the Great Bear.

Zeus was in love with a beautiful nymph named Callisto, but had to transform her into a bear to conceal her from Hera. When Hera tricked Artemis into hunting the bear, Zeus saved Callisto by placing her in the heavens.

The Greeks saw the heavens like this:

Here's an art project that will help you to make your own constellations. For a star lamp, you'll need:

○ a flashlight

○ aluminum foil

○ a permanent marker

○ a fine-tipped pen or pencil

○ some kind of open-topped, cylindrical container larger than your flashlight (a coffee can, oatmeal box, toy bucket, etc.)

○ tape

A note on flashlights: I found that a small, non-LED pocket flashlight worked best for me, Junior Geniuses. Bigger flashlights have a more uneven beam, while flashlights with multiple LEDs produced a weird, scattered image. Experiment a bit to see what kind of light gives the best results.

First, mount the flashlight inside the container, pointing up. Depending on the container, it might be easiest to punch a hole in the bottom that will hold the flashlight in place, or use duct tape. For mine, I used an ancient Greek technique: Fill the container with a few inches of Lego bricks to keep the flashlight in place.

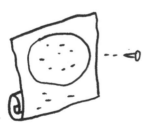

With the marker, trace the top of the container onto a sheet of the aluminum foil so you know how big your drawing surface is.

Pick your favorite constellation, and look it up online to find its mythological backstory and—more important—a good image of it. Use the marker to copy

the constellation's pattern onto the foil. Then poke a hole in each "star" using a pushpin or fine-tipped pen. Foil tears easily, so be supercareful!

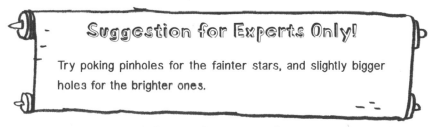

Suggestion for Experts Only!

Try poking pinholes for the fainter stars, and slightly bigger holes for the brighter ones.

Tape your foil over the top of the container *upside down* (so the constellation is backward). If your container is thin enough that light shines out through the sides, line the sides with foil as well.

Now take your star lamp into a completely dark place and let your constellation shine onto the ceiling. You are like the Zeus of this closet or bathroom! Try not to let all the power go to your head.

FOURTH PERIOD

Deities and Demigods

The Olympians are definitely the most important Greek gods and the ones they told the most stories about. But their full roll call of immortals wasn't limited to just twelve. (Okay, *fine*, fourteen!)

In fact, the Greeks saw divine figures everywhere in the world around them, from the fiery sun overhead to the smallest brook. Every tree was a nymph, every pond a naiad. Even abstract ideas like "modesty," "boldness," and "making excuses" got converted into personified spirits. (Aidos, Thrasos, and Prophasis, if you were wondering.)

But have no fear, Junior Geniuses. (Phrike: goddess of fear and trembling.) With a little hard work (Ponos: god of toil) you can keep track of all these deities and demigods. This I swear! (Horkos: god of oaths.)

Look! Up in the Sky!

The Greek sky gods seem like they'd have it pretty easy up there, right? Lots of light, great view, no traffic. But life wasn't always heavenly for them. Even being the sun or the moon, it turns out, can have its ups and downs.

HELIOS The charioteer of the sun had a mortal son named Phaethon who was always bragging to his friends that his dad drove the sun. (*"Sure* he does, Phaethon," they probably told him at recess.) Phaethon endlessly begged his father to let him have a turn behind the wheel, and finally, in a moment of weakness, Helios gave in. As you might have guessed, Phaethon was a terrible driver. He lost control of Helios's four horses almost immediately. They galloped so high that the earth froze, and then they plummeted so close to the ground that the fields scorched. Zeus finally had to zap Phaethon with a thunderbolt to end his rampage. His sisters, the Heliades, stood by the river where he had fallen and wept so long that Zeus changed them into poplar trees that dripped tears of amber. **MORAL:** Get your learner's permit before you try to drive, kids!

SELENE The goddess of the moon had a weird love life. As she passed across the heavens each night, she couldn't help noticing a handsome shepherd-king named Endymion sleeping in a cave on Mount Latmus. But every time he woke up, she lost interest! Finally she persuaded Zeus to grant him endless sleep, so she could come kiss him with her moonbeams any time she wanted but not actually have to hang out or talk or anything. **MORAL:** Your girlfriend is nuts, Endymion, wake up! Oh, that's right, you can't.

EOS Selene got off easy compared to Eos, the goddess of the dawn. Eos admired two handsome Trojan princes named Tithonus and Ganymede, and she whisked them away to her palace in the east. When Zeus took Ganymede away to become the new cupbearer of Olympus, Eos asked that Tithonus be granted eternal life so he could stay with her forever. Zeus agreed . . . but Eos forgot to ask for eternal youth as well! Tithonus couldn't die, but he got so old that he finally shriveled up into a grass-hopper, chirping away in her bedroom forever. **MORAL:** The gods are trying to swindle you, so make sure you read the fine print!

BOREAS NORTH WIND

EURUS UNLUCKY EAST WIND

N

W

E

THE FOUR WINDS The four winds, or Anemoi, were the sons of Eos, and to the Greeks, they each had a very different personality. They were Boreas, the icy north wind; Notus, the humid south wind; Zephyrus, the gentle west wind; and Eurus, the unlucky east wind. In later myths, the winds were kept locked up on the floating island of the storm god Aeolus. Sometimes he would even stuff them into a big bag and let visitors borrow them if they needed wind power. **MORAL:** "Free as the wind"? Yeah, right.

ZEPHYRUS GENTLE WEST WIND

NOTUS SOUTH WIND RAIN

Sisters Are Doin' It for Themselves

The Greeks imagined the four winds as male gods, but most of the other team-ups in their mythology were (a) trios, and (b) women. These can get confusing, so here's a field guide to telling these triple goddesses apart.

	Greek Word	Roman Word	Members
THE FATES	Moirai	Parcae	CLOTHO (spins) LACHESIS (measures) ATROPOS (cuts)
THE GRACES	Charites	Gratiae	AGLAEA (splendor) EUPHROSYNE (mirth) THALIA (cheer)
THE HOURS	Horai	Horae	THALLO (spring) AUXO (summer) CARPO (autumn)
THE FURIES	Erinyes	Dirae	ALECTO (anger) TISIPHONE (vengeance) MEGAERA (jealousy)
THE GRAY SISTERS	Graiai	Graiae	DEINO (dread) ENYO (horror) PEMPHREDO (terror)

THE FATES

Job	Tip for Identifying
Weaving mortal life, from birth to death	Super interested in thread
Attending Aphrodite as goddesses of charm and beauty	Very happy, very naked
Guarding the cloud-gates of Olympus, ordering seasons and stars	Always carry plants and flowers around
Punishing mortals who lied or murdered	Carry whips studded with brass, have bat wings and creepy bloodshot eyes
Being old, even when they were young	All share one eye and one tooth

Not Fooling Anyone

The Greeks were so afraid of the Furies that they refused to call them by their real names—instead, they tried to appease them by calling them the Eumenides—the "Kindly Ones."

The Muses are easier to recognize as long as you can count past three: there are nine of them! They were the daughters of Zeus and Mnemosyne, the Titaness of memory, and each Muse oversaw one of the arts or sciences.

	Calliope	Epic poetry
	Clio	History
	Erato	Love poetry
	Euterpe	Song
	Melpomene	Tragedy
	Polyhymnia	Hymns
	Terpsichore	Dance
	Thalia	Comedy
	Urania	Astronomy

Apollo brought them down from the wild mountains to his temple at Delphi, where he led them in song and dance.

Into the Woods

The Muses weren't the only gods who wandered the forests and mountains. In Greek stories, the countryside was a wild, exciting place, without the law and order that ruled in the cities. Out in the wilderness, anything could happen.

The great god of the wild was Pan, the son of Hermes. The other Greek gods were always described as incredibly, radiantly good-looking, like movie stars only *for real*, without the hair weaves and bronzer. Pan, on the other hand, was nobody's physical ideal.

When he was born, he was so ugly that even his mother screamed and ran away. Hermes took him to

TWO small HORNS
POINTY EARS
HAD THIS BEARD EVEN AS A BABY
SHAGGY BLACK HAIR EVERYWHERE! UGH.
GOAT LEGS

Olympus, where he won the gods over with his crude charm, but he soon decided he preferred the hills of Arcadia, where his hobbies included:

- **Sleeping all day**

- **Hunting**

- **Screaming to frighten passersby—which is where we get our word "panic"**

I've Never Heard Satyr News

Pan is the only one of the Greek gods—all immortal, of course—to have a myth about his death! According to the historian Plutarch, a sailor named Thamus once heard a mysterious voice from the island of Paxi call to him that, when he got to port, he should tell everyone that the great god Pan was dead. Plutarch doesn't consider the possibility that someone was just playing an incredibly elaborate prank on poor Thamus.

By night, Pan became the first DJ, playing a flute of his own invention, the panpipe, for crowds of dancing nymphs.

Valley Girls

Nymphs were minor nature deities who—luckily for Pan—took the form of beautiful young girls. Some were immortal, but others were just very, *very* long-lived. The Greek poet Hesiod did the math this way:

1 crow lifetime = 9 human generations

1 stag lifetime = 4 crow lifetimes

1 raven lifetime = 3 stag lifetimes

1 phoenix lifetime = 9 raven lifetimes

 1 nymph lifetime = 10 phoenix lifetimes

If a human generation is 20 years long, that means a nymph can live 194,400 years!

Nymphs were classified by the natural features they represented, as illustrated below.

As you can see, it was hard to go outside at all without tripping over a nymph or two. Nymphs could dance and play in the form of beautiful young women, but they were also firmly bound to their tree or mountain or river. If the tree died or the pond dried up, the nymph would die as well. Greek woodcutters were supposed to ask the nymph's permission before cutting down her tree, or else they'd face the wrath of the gods.

Just Desserts

Erysichthon, the king of Thessaly, foolishly ordered his men to chop down a grove sacred to Demeter. When they refused to cut down a huge oak that was Demeter's favorite, he grabbed an ax and cut down the sacred tree himself, killing a dryad in the process. As she died, she cursed Erysichthon with a terrible hunger that only grew worse the more he ate. In the end he became so hungry that he ate himself!

Most of the classical myths about nymphs are love stories, but they don't always end happily. They have lots of shape-changing though!

LIMNIAD
LAKE NYMPH

OREAD
MOUNTAIN NYMPH

NEPHELAE
CLOUD NYMPH

NAPAEA
VALLEY NYMPH

ALSEID
GROVE NYMPH

LEMONIAD
MEADOW NYMPH

NEREID
SEA NYMPH

THE NAIAD WHO TURNED INTO HEADWEAR

The god Apollo fell in love with the river god's beautiful

daughter Daphne, but she was afraid and ran away from him. At the last moment, she prayed to Gaea, who transformed her into a laurel tree. Apollo watched as the bark closed over her skin; then he sadly gathered a few of her leaves to wear as a garland.

From that time on, Apollo always wore laurel leaves on his head, and they were given to honor the winners at ancient Greek games like the Olympics.

THE OREAD WHO TURNED INTO A DISEMBODIED VOICE

Echo was a chatty nymph who would distract Hera with endless stories while Zeus was off partying with the other nymphs. Hera got wise to Echo's tricks and cursed her so that she could only repeat the words of others. Eventually she wasted away in loneliness, leaving only her voice mimicking visitors to the woods and hills. (This is the source of our word "echo," of course.)

THE NYMPH WHO TURNED INTO A MUSICAL INSTRUMENT

Syrinx was a nymph who, like her mistress Artemis, had made a vow of chastity. One day as Pan was chasing her, she realized she was about to be caught, so she asked a river nymph to transform her into a hollow reed by the water's edge. Pan couldn't find her, so he cut down a whole patch of the reeds and made them into a flute, which he named the *syrinx* in her honor. (Our modern word "syringe," a hollow tube used by doctors, also comes from poor Syrinx.)

THE NEREID WHO TURNED INTO FIRE, A LION, AN OCTOPUS, AND SOME OTHER STUFF, I FORGET

It had been prophesied that the son of the sea nymph Thetis would grow up to be even greater than his father, so a worried Zeus wanted to make sure she married a mortal man, not a god! She turned down Peleus, the king of Aegina, when he proposed marriage, but Peleus wasn't the type to take no for an answer. His plan was to hold on to her so tightly that she couldn't escape with her shape-changing powers. She changed into fire, water, and wind, a tree and then a bird, then a tiger, a lioness, a serpent, and an octopus, but Peleus refused to let go until she agreed to marry him. (This is also how I wound up with my wife, Junior Geniuses. She's got some grip!) Their son turned out to be the almost-invulnerable Achilles.

All Wet

Thetis was one of the fifty beautiful sea nymphs who lived in a silvery underwater cavern with their parents, Nereus and Doris. Nereus was the "Old Man of the Sea," a seaweed-bearded god who herded Poseidon's seals for him.

There were other minor sea gods as well. Triton lived with his parents, Poseidon and Amphitrite, in their golden palace beneath the Aegean Sea. He had a dolphin tail, and rode a sea monster over the waves, which he could calm or raise up by blowing on the conch-shell trumpet he carried.

Proteus was a sea god who could foretell the future—but only if you could pin him down. He was a shape-shifter, which is where we get our word "protean," meaning "versatile" or "changeable." In fact, he was the one who advised Peleus on how to woo Thetis.

The strangest sea god was Glaucus. He was just a mortal fisherman working his nets in Greece when he discovered a type of sea grass that would bring dead fish back to life. Curious, he tried eating it himself. Not only did the herb make him immortal, it made him grow fins and gills! He jumped into the sea and never returned, becoming the protector of sailors and fishermen menaced by storms.

Darker Gods

Nyx, the Greek goddess of night, was a shadowy winged figure sometimes said to be older even than Gaea herself. Even Zeus stood in awe of her. She dwelled in the darkness of Hades with her children, Thanatos and the Keres. Thanatos was the god of peaceful death, a corpse-faced god who carried a scythe and wore armor and a black cloak. The Roman poet Ovid imagined him always watching an hourglass, so he could tell when it was time to escort a new victim down to the underworld.

His sisters, the Keres, were bloodthirsty goddesses of slaughter, with gleaming teeth and claws. Hecate, the goddess of witchcraft and the crossroads, joined these gods in attending Hades on his dark throne.

Pop Quiz!

The Greek sorceress Circe, from Homer's *Odyssey*, was sometimes said to be the daughter of Hecate. Circe's big claim to fame is changing Odysseus's crew into what?

Nyx's other children, Hypnos (god of sleep) and Morpheus (god of dreams), lived in a cave so far in the east that the sun's rays never reached them. It was surrounded by poppies and other sleep-inducing herbs. They slept on downy-soft couches of ebony and sable, and there wasn't even a gate on their palace, because the squeaking of the hinges might wake them up.

Speaking of which: WAKE UP, CLASS!

It's time for lunch.

LUNCH

The Greek gods normally ate only nectar and ambrosia, but when they brown-bagged it instead, bad things happened. King Tantalus of Phrygia once served the gods meat that actually came from his son Pelops, whom he'd killed and boiled!

But here's a recipe for a can't-miss snack idea inspired by the Trojan horse. Remember the Trojan horse? The Mycenaean Greek army at Troy fought for years but couldn't breach the city's great walls. Finally they built a giant wooden horse and left it before the gates of Troy. The Trojans took it as a gift of surrender and rolled the horse into the city. Bad idea! By night, while Troy was partying, a team of Greeks stole out of the hollow horse and opened the city gates. The Greek fleet had returned and easily took the city, ending the war.

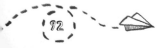

These Trojan horses are homemade, not Homer-made! They're less dangerous—as long as you make sure you get a grown-up to help with the oven and whatnot—but more delicious. The horses are sugar cookies, and the Greek soldiers hidden inside are miniature M&M's. (The *M* is for "Mycenaeans"!)

Trojan Treats

Ingredients

3 1/4 cups flour

1 1/2 teaspoons baking powder

1/2 teaspoon salt

2 1/2 sticks unsalted butter, softened

1 cup sugar

1 egg

1 tablespoon milk

2 1/2 teaspoons vanilla extract

1/4 teaspoon grated lemon zest (the yellow part of the peel)—optional

Not Technically Ingredients, But You Also Need

1 horse-shaped cookie cutter. The bigger the better! 4–5" across is best.

Frosting

1/2 cup powdered sugar

2 teaspoons milk

Teeny Tiny Greek Army

1 tube M&M's Minis (not regular M&M's)

Directions

1. In a medium bowl, whisk together the flour, baking powder, and salt.

2. In a different bowl, beat the butter and sugar together on medium speed.

3. Add the egg, milk, vanilla, and lemon zest to the butter mixture, and beat until well combined.

4. Carefully stir the flour mixture into the butter mixture and blend well.

5. Divide the dough in half, and roll out each half until it's about ¼-inch thick. (For kids, this is easiest between two pieces of parchment paper, if you have any.)

6. Refrigerate the dough on baking trays until it's firm—maybe half an hour. Use a sundial for extra Greek authenticity!

7. Preheat the oven to 375°.

8. When the dough has chilled, cut out horse shapes and carefully transfer them to a cookie sheet. Bake until the little ears and hooves and tails are *just* starting to darken—around 7–9 minutes.

9. Make the frosting by combining the powdered sugar and milk in a resealable plastic bag.

10. Each horse is built out of three cookies: two sides and a middle. If your cookies have tails, cut the tail off

both side cookies. Cut the legs and ears off the middle cookie, and also cut a little window out of the middle horse's body, big enough to drop in a few candies. If you have a square or rectangular cookie cutter that's small enough, use that. Do all this before the cookies cool and get brittle!

11. Cut out one corner of the frosting bag to make a little dispenser, and pipe frosting onto the two side cookies. Press the middle cookie onto one side cookie, put a few M&M's in the secret compartment, then attach the other side cookie with more frosting-glue.

12. Sack the great city of Troy by night. Watch the topless towers of Ilium burn as Priam's royal family is killed and enslaved. All for a woman! Enjoy your cookies.

FIFTH PERIOD

Superheroes

The ancient Greeks told epic stories about amazing men and women who lived in recent memory, just a few generations before their own. Some had divine blood in their veins; others were just taught and protected by the gods. Like today's comic book heroes, they had:

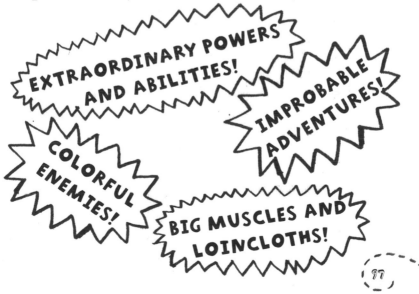

EXTRAORDINARY POWERS AND ABILITIES!

IMPROBABLE ADVENTURES!

COLORFUL ENEMIES!

BIG MUSCLES AND LOINCLOTHS!

Secret Origins

Like comic-book heroes, Greek heroes sometimes had humble—or downright weird—backgrounds. The great hunter Orion was the son of King Hyrieus, who once offered hospitality to three gods: Zeus, Hermes, and Poseidon. When they asked the king if they could grant him one wish, Hyrieus asked for a son. The gods agreed, and all three peed into a bull's hide(!), which they told Hyrieus to bury in the ground. Nine months later, the king dug up the hide and found a baby boy in it. That's why he named his son Orion, meaning "urine."

More Powerful Than a Locomotive

The greatest of all the Greek heroes was Heracles. Even as an infant, he was strong enough to strangle two snakes that had crawled into his cradle. His parents were Zeus and the mortal woman Alcmene, so Hera hated him terribly. She finally drove Heracles so mad that he killed his own children. In penance, he had to perform ten incredibly difficult labors for his cousin and rival, King Eurystheus.

Unsung Heroes

Not every hero from the Race of Heroes was a burly he-man like Heracles. Let's not forget Perdix, who invented the saw one day while looking at the skeleton of a fish. Or Pelasgos, who taught people to eat acorns instead of just grass and leaves. Nice one, Pelasgos.

In some myths, Heracles's strength makes him a bit of a lunkhead. His favorite weapon was a big olive-wood club, after all. And when the sun was too hot or the sea too choppy, he'd try to fix things by shooting arrows at it. But when Heracles performed his famous ten labors for Eurystheus, he actually proved himself to be a pretty clever problem solver.

How to Solve Problems ... the Heracles Way!

LABOR 1

The Mission ⇨ Kill the enormous Nemean lion

The Problem ⇨ The lion's hide was impenetrable to stone or metal.

Heracles's Solution ⇨ Heracles strangled it with his bare hands, even though it bit off one of his fingers!

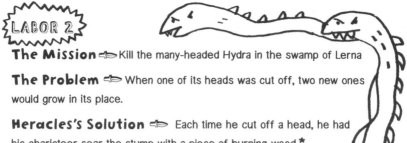

LABOR 2

The Mission ⇨ Kill the many-headed Hydra in the swamp of Lerna

The Problem ⇨ When one of its heads was cut off, two new ones would grow in its place.

Heracles's Solution ⇨ Each time he cut off a head, he had his charioteer sear the stump with a piece of burning wood.*

LABOR 3

The Mission ⇨ Capture the golden-horned Cerynean hind

The Problem ⇨ This deer was so fast it could outrun an arrow.

Heracles's Solution ⇨ He tracked the deer for a full year, and then trapped it in a net while it slept.

LABOR 4

The Mission ⇨ Capture the fierce Erymanthian boar

The Problem ⇨ The much-feared boar was in a wild rage.

Heracles's Solution ⇨ He drove it into snow. Then, when it was trapped in a drift, he hopped on its back and chained it.

The Mission ⇨ Clean the stables of King Augeas

The Problem ⇨ Thirty years of poop from 1,000 cows to be cleaned in a single day?!

Heracles's Solution ⇨ He diverted two rivers to "flush" out the filthy stables.*

The Mission ⇨ Rid the Stymphalian marsh of its vicious birds

The Problem ⇨ The man-eating birds attacked with bronze beaks, claws, and feathers.

Heracles's Solution ⇨ He frightened the birds by shaking a deafening rattle made for him by Hephaestus.

The Mission ⇨ Capture the Cretan bull

The Problem ⇨ It ravaged the countryside breathing scorching flames.

Heracles's Solution ⇨ He throttled the bull from behind until it was too weak to resist.

LABOR 8

The Mission ⇨ Steal the mares of the cruel King Diomedes

The Problem ⇨ These savage horses fed on human flesh.

Heracles's Solution ⇨ He trapped them by flooding their pasture, then calmed them by feeding their master to them!

LABOR 9

The Mission ⇨ Retrieve the golden belt of Queen Hippolyta

The Problem ⇨ Hippolyta was queen of the warlike Amazons; the belt was a prized gift from Ares.

Heracles's Solution ⇨ He looked so good that an impressed Hippolyta offered him the belt as a love token.

LABOR 10

The Mission ⇨ Bring back the cattle of Geryon

The Problem ⇨ Geryon was a monstrous giant with three mighty bodies.

Heracles's Solution ⇨ He fired a single arrow into Geryon's side so hard that it pierced all three bodies.

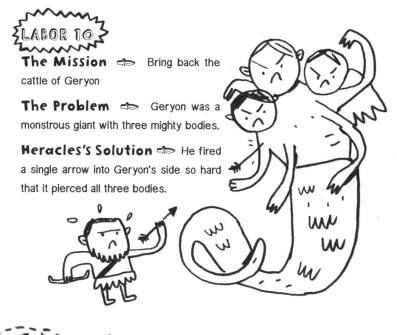

Pop Quiz!

Annoyed that Heracles was doing so well against the Hydra, Hera sent a giant crab to attack him at the same time! When Heracles crushed the crab, Hera sadly placed its body in the heavens—as which sign of the Zodiac?

At this point, eight years had passed and Heracles should have been done, but King Eurystheus got greedy. He claimed that two of those labors (the ones marked with asterisks) shouldn't count, since Heracles had outside help. (In one case, his charioteer, and in the other case, two rivers.) So he sent Heracles out on two more errands, the most difficult ones of all.

LABOR 11

The Mission ⇔ Fetch the golden apples of the Hesperides

The Problem ⇔ Hera's prized fruit was guarded by the hundred-headed dragon, Ladon.

Heracles's Solution ⇔ He held up the heavens while mighty Atlas picked the apples, then tricked Atlas into resuming his burden.

Here was the trick: He told Atlas, "Okay, I'll hold up the sky from now on. But can you take over for just one second while I fold my cloak into a pad on my back?" Atlas agreed, and Heracles walked away laughing. So basically Atlas was pretty gullible.

LABOR 12

The Mission ⇨ Bring three-headed Cerberus up from Tartarus

The Problem ⇨ Getting to the land of the dead *and* stealing its watchdog? Wow.

Heracles's Solution ⇨ He intimidated Charon, the boatman of Hades, with a fierce scowl, and then persuaded Hades to let him borrow Cerberus if he could subdue it in combat—which he did.

King Eurystheus was so surprised and terrified when Heracles walked into his court carrying Cerberus that he jumped headfirst into a big jar. He agreed to release Heracles from servitude if Heracles promised to return Cerberus to Hades—*as soon as possible!*

Don't Leave Home Without It!

For a modern-day hero to meet all the challenges faced by the Greek heroes, he or she would need a pretty impressive utility belt of equipment. Here are some of the must-haves for the well-dressed hero.

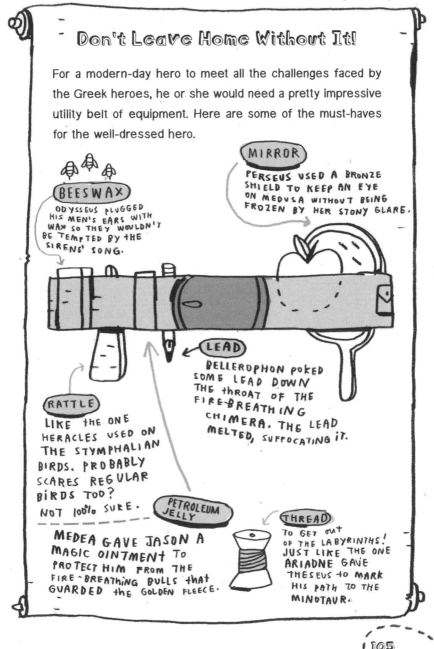

MIRROR

PERSEUS USED A BRONZE SHIELD TO KEEP AN EYE ON MEDUSA WITHOUT BEING FROZEN BY HER STONY GLARE.

BEESWAX

ODYSSEUS PLUGGED HIS MEN'S EARS WITH WAX SO THEY WOULDN'T BE TEMPTED BY THE SIRENS' SONG.

LEAD

BELLEROPHON POKED SOME LEAD DOWN THE THROAT OF THE FIRE-BREATHING CHIMERA. THE LEAD MELTED, SUFFOCATING IT.

RATTLE

LIKE THE ONE HERACLES USED ON THE STYMPHALIAN BIRDS. PROBABLY SCARES REGULAR BIRDS TOO? NOT 100% SURE.

PETROLEUM JELLY

MEDEA GAVE JASON A MAGIC OINTMENT TO PROTECT HIM FROM THE FIRE-BREATHING BULLS THAT GUARDED THE GOLDEN FLEECE.

THREAD

TO GET OUT OF THE LABYRINTHS! JUST LIKE THE ONE ARIADNE GAVE THESEUS TO MARK HIS PATH TO THE MINOTAUR.

Truth, Justice, and the Athenian Way

Like their comic-book descendants, the Greek heroes often joined up to form superheroic team-ups, the ancient equivalent of the Justice League or the Avengers. Dozens of heroes banded together for adventures like the Calydonian Boar Hunt or the Trojan War. But the most famous team-up of them all was the Quest for the Golden Fleece.

Once upon a time, in the faraway kingdom of Iolcus, King Aeson was overthrown by his power-hungry half brother, Pelias. Pelias even tried to kill Aeson's baby son Jason, but Jason was smuggled out of the city to Mount Pelion, where he was raised by Chiron the centaur.

Jason returned to Iolcus as a young man, but lost one of his sandals crossing a river. An oracle had warned Pelias that he would be killed by a one-sandaled man, so Pelias was on his guard. When Jason boldly claimed his father's throne, Pelias tried to get rid of him by sending

him off on a hopeless quest: to recover the magic ram's skin called the Golden Fleece.

Jason accepted, but decided to take no chances. He ordered the construction of a ship with fifty oars, and Athena herself carved its prow out of a magical piece of wood cut from Zeus's sacred oak at Dodona. This allowed the ship to talk and prophesy! Jason named his ship the *Argo* and assembled fifty of the world's greatest heroes to sail with him to Colchis. They were called the *Argo*-sailors, or, in Greek, "Argonauts."

Argonauts, Assemble!

The Greeks could never agree on the exact roll call of the Argonauts, with ninety or so names appearing on various lists. Many of them were all-star heroes like Heracles, Theseus, Atalanta, and Meleager. Others were lesser-known names with special gifts, like Butes, the world's greatest beekeeper; Aethalides, who had a photographic memory; Lynceus, who had X-ray vision; and Euphemus, who could walk on water.

Once on the open sea, the *Argo* had to face a series of obstacles, each more challenging than the last.

STINKY WOMEN! On the island of Lemnos, the Argonauts were ensnared by a group of women who had been cursed by the goddess of Aphrodite with a terrible stench. When the men living on the island got revolted by the smell, the women angrily killed them, and hoped the Argonauts would replace their husbands. Heracles saved the tempted Argonauts by banging on the palace gates with his club and reminding them of their quest.

Crew Cut

Heracles never made it to Colchis, sadly. The talking prow of the *Argo* complained that the muscleman was too heavy for the voyage, so his shipmates sent him ashore at the Cape of Magnesia to get water . . . and then sailed off without him, ditching him there!

AN ARROGANT BOXER! Amycus, the king of Bebrycos, was a big jerk who challenged all visitors to his island to a boxing match. Amycus had muscles like boulders and even put metal spikes on his boxing gloves, but he was still defeated by the Argonaut Pollux, the boxing champion of the first Olympics.

A STARVING KING! King Phineus of Thrace had been cursed by Zeus with a pair of Harpies, monstrous bird-women who stole food from his table and pooped on the rest. (Yuck.) Calais and Zetes, winged sons of the west wind, chased them off, and Phineus told the Argonauts the secret of how to pass their next obstacle . . .

Giant Clashing Rocks! These huge stone cliffs would crush anything that passed between them. Thanks to Phineus, Jason knew what to do: He released a dove, knowing that if the dove made it through the passage, he should begin rowing immediately. The rocks crashed together on the dove's tail feathers, but it barely made it through. The Argonauts followed, rowing so hard that their oars bent like bows, and the *Argo* lost only the decoration on its stern when the rocks crashed together for the final time.

Really Nice Singing! The Sirens lived on small islands and lured sailors to a rocky death with their beautiful songs. But Orpheus, the world's greatest musician, played an even more beautiful song on his lyre so his shipmates could pass by in safety.

A Giant Robot! Talos was a man of bronze made by Hephaestus, and he was so huge that he could run around the vast island of Crete three times a day! Talos had a single vein of godly ichor running from his neck to his ankle that made him invulnerable, but the Argonauts tricked him into removing the nail that kept his vein shut, and he bled to death.

Eventually the *Argo* arrived at its destination, and King Aeetes of Colchis agreed to give Jason the Golden Fleece if he could perform a seemingly impossible task: plow a field using fire-breathing oxen, then sow it with dragon teeth. But the king's daughter Medea had been struck with one of Eros's arrows and fell in love with Jason, so she taught him all the tricks. For example, when he threw the dragon teeth into the field, Medea knew they would sprout into an army of warriors. She told Jason to throw a rock into the crowd. Not knowing where the rock had come from, the newborn warriors quickly killed each other!

Then Jason and Medea made their way to the thousand-coiled dragon that guarded the Golden Fleece. Medea put it to sleep with a powerful potion, and they escaped back to the *Argo* with the fleece.

Don't Rock the Boat!

Jason's life did not end as happily as his quest. He became king of Iolcus, but ten years later he tried to divorce Medea so that he could marry Glauce, a princess of Corinth, to ally their two countries. Medea was so angry that she gave Glauce a terrible wedding present: a white robe that burned Glauce to death when she tried it on. Medea even killed two of her own children! Jason was alone and unhappy for the rest of his life, sometimes sleeping under the beached hull of the *Argo*. One day the rotting stern collapsed, and he died.

SIGH!

Pocket Full of Kryptonite

Just like Superman, many superpowered folks from Greek myth had great strength but one mortal weakness. Inevitably, that weakness led to their downfall.

ACHILLES

Weakness: His mother, Thetis, dipped him in the River Styx as a baby to make him immortal, but she held him by his heel, which stayed dry (and vulnerable).

Wouldn't you know it? He was killed at Troy when Paris shot him in the heel with an arrow.

THE GIANTS

Weakness: An oracle told the Olympian gods that a rebellion of Giants would overthrow them—unless a mortal fought on their side.

Wouldn't you know it? Heracles joined the battle and killed six of the otherwise unbeatable Giants.

MELEAGER

Weakness: The Fates said he would live as long as a certain piece of wood was unconsumed by fire. So his mother snatched the wood out of the fire and hid it in a chest.

Wouldn't you know it? His mother got mad when he killed his uncles during the Calydonian Boar Hunt, so she threw the log back on the fire.

ALCYONEUS

Weakness: This Thracian giant was immortal—but not outside of his homeland, Pallene.

Wouldn't you know it? Heracles dragged him across the border, then killed him there.

CYGNUS

Weakness: This king who fought at Troy had been made invulnerable to weapons by his dad, Poseidon—but against *non*weapons, he was helpless.

Wouldn't you know it? When Achilles found that he couldn't kill Cycnus with a sword, he just smooshed him with a big rock.

ANTAEUS

Weakness: This half giant was the son of Gaea, so he was unbeatably strong—as long as he was touching his mother, the earth.

Wouldn't you know it? Heracles lifted him into the air and crushed him there.

You Too Can Be a Hero!

The heroes of Greek mythology had weaknesses of character as well—they weren't perfect by any means. In fact, here are some easy ways for you to be *more heroic* than these famed heroes!

Don't be a bad winner! After Odysseus escaped from the Cyclops Polyphemus, he taunted the Cyclops from his ship. This "nyah nyah!" angered Polyphemus's father, the god Poseidon, who sent stormy seas that kept Odysseus from getting home for *twenty years*!

Don't sulk in your room for months! The Greeks lost battle after battle during the Trojan War because the great Achilles sat sulking in his tent, refusing to fight. He was angry that his commander, Agamemnon, had stolen the beautiful princess Briseis from him.

Don't murder your piano teacher! As a boy, Heracles took music lessons from Linus, the son of Apollo himself. But when Linus scolded his technique, Heracles whacked the old man with his lyre, accidentally killing him.

Don't marry your mom! Even though an oracle had warned that he would kill his father and marry his mother, Oedipus married Jocasta—the widow of a man he had just killed, mind you!—without looking into her family history. Sure enough, she turned out to be his birth mother. Yuck. Oedipus blinded himself in grief.

Don't hunt entire species to extinction! The great Orion, hunting with the goddess Artemis on Crete, threatened to kill *every single animal on earth*. Wow. Gaea, concerned, sent a giant scorpion to sting Orion to death.

MUSIC CLASS

Originally, Junior Geniuses, the Greek myths were set to music. A singer called the rhapsode would chant the epic poems of Homer and others, sometimes accompanied by a lyre. Our modern word "music" even comes from the Muses, the nine Greek goddesses of the arts.

LYRE

The gods all enjoyed music, and Pan once had the nerve to challenge the god Apollo to a musical contest, *Greek Idol*–style. Pan played charmingly on his flute, but when it was Apollo's turn, he played so beautifully on his gem-covered ivory lyre that the contest judge, the mountain god Tmolus, immediately awarded the victory to Apollo. Watching the contest was King Midas, of "golden touch" fame, and he made the mistake of speaking up, saying that he preferred Pan, actually. An angry Apollo punished Midas's bad taste by turning his ears into donkey ears.

Midas tried to keep the humiliating ears a secret, but his barber saw them, of course, and *had* to tell someone. Finally the barber went to a riverbank and whispered "Midas has ass's ears!" into a hole in the ground. Unfortunately, the reeds that grew on that bank always  hissed "Midas has ass's ears!" when the wind blew past them, and Midas's secret was out!

The greatest mortal musician was Orpheus. When he sang, wild beasts would sit tamely to listen, and even trees and rocks would move to follow the music.

But Orpheus's story is a sad one. His beautiful bride, Eurydice, was killed on their wedding day by a poisonous snake, and Orpheus ventured into the underworld to bring her back. He used his lyre to charm the ferryman Charon and the dog Cerberus to allow him entry. Even the souls of the dead paused in their tortures to listen to his song. Hades was so moved that he allowed Eurydice to follow Orpheus out of his realm— as long as Orpheus never looked back at her until they were both in the sunlight.

But just as they were about to emerge from the underworld, Orpheus couldn't stand the suspense anymore and looked behind him, and he lost Eurydice forever.

Orpheus wandered the world grieving, and was finally torn to pieces by frenzied maenads, the followers of Dionysus. They threw his head into the river, and it floated downstream to the sea, still singing sadly. The Greek poet Pindar says that, to this day, you can see a grove of oak trees in Thrace that are still standing in the pattern they made as they danced to the song of Orpheus.

SIXTH PERIOD

Junior Geniuses: Do you ever hear your parents or other adults reminiscing about the "good old days"? Usually they just mean a time a few decades ago when gas was cheaper and they still understood what was going on in popular music. But the good old days must be longer ago than that—over 2,500 years ago, the ancient Greeks *already* thought they'd missed out on all the fun.

The Greek poet Hesiod wrote that the gods had created humankind in five different ages.

1. THE GOLDEN RACE, a perfect people created by Prometheus

2. THE SILVER RACE, destroyed by Zeus

3. THE BRONZE RACE, tough warriors who killed each other off

4. THE RACE OF HEROES, amazing men and women like Heracles

5. THE IRON RACE, the mean people of modern times.

So the next time a grown-up starts to tell you everything that's wrong with "kids today," just remember that Greek parents were making the same complaints . . . seven hundred years BC!

In this class, Junior Geniuses, we're going to meet the most interesting mortals in Greek mythology. Some of the best stories in Greek myth aren't about gods and heroes and monsters, but about regular Joes. Just like in real life.

Boast Stories

A dumb thing to do if you're a mortal in a Greek myth is to start telling the gods you're better than they are. The Greeks called this hubris (HYOO-bris), or extreme arrogance, and it ends badly, every time.

AJAX THE LESSER

Boast ⇨   After he survived a shipwreck caused by Athena, he laughed and said that even the gods couldn't destroy him.

Punishment ⇨   Poseidon crashed his trident down on the rock Ajax was clinging to, and Ajax drowned in the sea.

NIOBE

Boast ⇨   Had fourteen children, so she laughed at Leto, who only had two.

Punishment ⇨   Leto's two children were . . . Apollo and Artemis. Oops. Apollo killed Niobe's seven sons and Artemis killed her seven daughters. Niobe turned to stone—the Weeping Rock still visible today in Mount Sipylus is Niobe crying for her children.

ALCYONE AND CEYX

Boast ⇨ This couple was so happy that they called each other "Zeus" and "Hera" as pet names.

Punishment ⇨ Zeus, not amused, threw a thunderbolt at Ceyx's ship, drowning him. A grieving Alcyone threw herself into the sea.

CASSIOPEIA

Boast ⇨ Claimed that she *and* her daughter Andromeda were more beautiful than the nereids of the sea.

Punishment ⇨ The nereids' dad, Poseidon, sent the sea monster Cetus to destroy Cassiopeia's kingdom.

KING SALMONEUS

Boast ⇨ Drove around town dragging noisy bronze kettles behind his chariot and throwing torches at his subjects, claiming to wield the power of the "thunder" and "lightning," just like Zeus.

Punishment ⇨ Zeus got fed up with this dork and threw down a *real* thunderbolt, which killed Salmoneus and burned down his entire city.

Ain't No Mountain High Enough

The ultimate braggarts in Greek myth were Otus and Ephialtes, two sons of Poseidon who were already nine fathoms (fifty-four feet!) tall by the time they turned nine. They decided to overthrow the gods by stacking up three mountains so they could climb to heaven. At first their campaign was successful—they even trapped Ares inside a bronze jar for a full year! In the end, Artemis tricked them by appearing as a beautiful white doe. Both brothers tried to throw a spear at the deer as she darted between them—and ended up spearing each other.

But the gods were fickle, and would punish mortals for lots of other infractions as well. Here's a partial list of the big DON'Ts.

DON'T Stiff Your Workers, or You'll Get Barfed on by a Sea Monster Laomedon of Troy refused to pay the two workers who had built his city's high walls. Unfortunately, the two workers were Poseidon and Apollo, who had been briefly banished from Olympus. In punishment, Apollo brought a plague down on Troy, and Poseidon sent a gross sea monster, which spewed seawater all over the people's fields.

DON'T Be a Peeping Tom, or Your Pets Will Eat You Hunting in the woods one day, Actaeon came across the goddess Artemis bathing in a stream. Artemis angrily changed him into a stag, and he was devoured by his own fifty hounds.

DON'T Arrive Late to a Wedding, or You'll Be Slow Forever A woman named Chelone was the only mortal who didn't show up at Zeus's wedding to Hera. So Hermes knocked the lazy woman's house into a river and transformed her into a tortoise.

DON'T Kidnap Little Boys, or You'll Need Gardeners for Your Pirate Ship A band of Tyrrhenian pirates once captured the young god Dionysus, thinking he was a prince they could sell into slavery. The wine god caused grapevines to sprout and cover their ship, and when they tried to escape into the sea, he turned them into dolphins.

Prophet Ability

Despite being mortal, many of the men and women in Greek myths had access to the divine knowledge of the gods. They were called oracles or seers, and they had really weird lives.

TIRESIAS This blind prophet of Thebes, out for a walk one day, passed a pair of snakes and whacked them with his stick. Annoyed, Hera turned him into a woman for seven years. He, as a she, even had a few kids.

MELAMPUS Luckily, this soothsayer of Pylos was nicer to snakes. One day he found a mother snake that had been run over by a cart, so he raised her orphaned babies himself. In gratitude, they licked his ears so he could understand the speech of animals.

POLYIDUS This seer found the missing prince Glaucus of Minos, who had fallen into a big jar of honey and died. Polyidus brought Glaucus back to life, but the king demanded he also teach Glaucus the gift of prophecy. He did so, but right before he left, Polyidus asked Glaucus to spit in his mouth. (Uh, okay.) When he did, Glaucus forgot all he'd learned.

CASSANDRA Apollo gave this Trojan princess the gift of prophecy as a reward for her great beauty. (Wait, how is that fair?) But when she rejected his advances, he

cursed her that her predictions would always be true . . . but no one would ever believe them.

AMPHIARAUS Zeus made this hero a great oracle, which meant that when he joined the doomed war party called the Seven Against Thebes, he already *knew* he was going to die on the battlefield. Bummer.

Like a Challenge?

Because game shows and reality shows hadn't been invented yet, the Greeks liked to tell stories about epic contests, especially if they involved mortals facing off against the gods.

THE PIERIDES VS THE MUSES

The nine daughters of King Pierus once challenged the Muses to a singing contest. The judges were nymphs who declared the Muses the winners, but the Pierides chattered and complained about the verdict, so the Muses turned them into magpies.

Winner: the Muses

OENOMAUS VS PELOPS

King Oenomaus had been warned by an oracle that his son-in-law would kill him, so anyone who wanted to marry his daughter had to beat him in a chariot race first. Twelve suitors had already died trying to outrace Oenomaus, and their heads hung on his palace walls. Pelops cleverly replaced the bronze pins on Oenomaus's chariot wheels with wax copies, and the king's chariot broke apart just as he was about to pass Pelops.

Winner: Pelops (by cheating)

ARACHNE 🌀 ATHENA

Arachne, a princess of Lydia, was such a masterful weaver that she challenged Athena herself, the goddess who had *invented* weaving, to a contest. Arachne's final tapestry was beautiful, but to tease Athena, she had filled it with images making fun of the gods. Athena angrily turned her into a spider, which today we still call arachnids.

Winner: Athena (by disqualification)

ATALANTA <ins>VS</ins> HIPPOMENES

Atalanta was a great huntress, having been raised by a she-bear when her father left her on a mountaintop to die. After returning to her father's kingdom, she said she would only marry a man who could beat her in a footrace, because she knew she was as swift as any challenger. Finally Hippomenes tricked her by throwing golden apples in her path during their race. Atalanta couldn't help slowing down to grab the beautiful fruit, and Hippomenes narrowly beat her to the finish line. They lived happily ever after, of course.

Winner: Hippomenes (by cheating)

HERA <ins>VS</ins> ATHENA <ins>VS</ins> APHRODITE

Speaking of golden apples: Eris, the goddess of discord, once threw an apple reading "to the fairest" between Hera, Athena, and Aphrodite, and they began to argue over which of them was the most beautiful of the three. They asked Paris of Troy to judge. Hera offered him a royal throne, Athena offered him greatness in war, and Aphrodite offered the love of the world's most beautiful woman.

Winner: Aphrodite

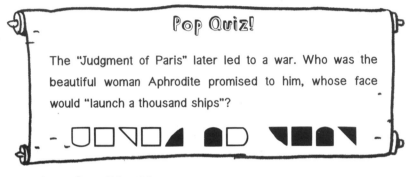

Pop Quiz!

The "Judgment of Paris" later led to a war. Who was the beautiful woman Aphrodite promised to him, whose face would "launch a thousand ships"?

Mushy Stuff

Most of the stories of the Greek gods aren't terribly romantic. Zeus disguises as something to romance some unsuspecting mortal woman, end of story.

Mortal Beauty	Zeus Disguises as . . .
Europa	a white bull
Leda	a swan
Danae	a shower of gold
Callisto	Artemis
Aegina	an eagle
Alcmene	her husband!

Classy, Zeus. But some of the Greek myths about *mortal* lovers are surprisingly sweet! (Okay, many are weird. But some are sweet!)

BAUCIS + PHILEMON This old couple offered hospitality to two travelers—and realized, when the travelers' cups kept magically refilling, that they were Zeus and Hermes! In repayment for their kindness, the gods allowed them to die peacefully together, and then transformed them into two intertwined trees.

ODYSSEUS + PENELOPE Penelope had many suitors when her husband, Odysseus, took *decades* to return home from Troy. (Not 100 percent his fault! Poseidon was mad at him. See page 114.) She promised to marry one of them as soon as she finished weaving a death shroud for her father-in-law. Then, for three years, she spent every night unraveling the day's weaving. Finally she held a banquet and said she'd marry whichever man could duplicate her husband's most amazing feat: shooting an arrow through the rings of twelve axes lined up. All failed, but then a lowly beggar performed the feat easily. It was Odysseus in disguise, returned home in the nick of time!

PYGMALION + GALATEA

Pygmalion was a sculptor who carved an ivory statue of a woman so beautiful that he fell in love with his own work. He sadly prayed that Aphrodite would lead him to a woman as lovely as the one he had made. Returning to his studio, he found the statue had come to life, and the two were married.

NARCISSUS + NARCISSUS The nymph Echo loved the handsome Narcissus, but Hera had cursed her so that she could only use her voice to repeat others (see page 86). For his part, Narcissus became obsessed with a beautiful image he saw in a forest pool, not realizing that it was his own reflection!

Echo could only watch helplessly as Narcissus sadly wasted away by the pool. Eventually the gods took pity and turned him into a white flower, which we still call the narcissus today.

Junior Geniuses of the Bronze Age

Odysses wasn't just a romantic action hero—he was also a big brain. In fact, he's number three on my ultra-scientific countdown of the Smartest People in Greek Mythology.

Mental Feats:

◦ **TRICKED ACHILLES** Achilles tried to dodge the Trojan War by disguising himself as a woman in the court of King Lycomedes. Odysseus discovered Achilles's whereabouts by giving the king's daughters gifts, including a sword and shield, then having his men blow trumpets as if announcing an attack. Out charged Achilles with the sword and shield!

○ **INVENTED THE TROJAN HORSE** The wooden horse that ended the Trojan War (see page 91) was Odysseus's bright idea.

○ **DEFEATED A CYCLOPS WITH WORDPLAY** When captured by the Cyclops Polyphemus, Odysseus claimed to be named Nobody. That way, when he blinded Polyphemus and the enraged Cyclops ran out of its cave to find help, it kept yelling things like "Nobody hurt me!" and "Nobody is trying to kill me!" So the other Cyclopes didn't come to his rescue.

Daedalus

Mental Feats:

○ **BUILT AND SOLVED THE WORLD'S MOST DIFFICULT MAZE** Daedalus built the famous Labyrinth of Crete to house the Minotaur. It was a maze of twisty passages so complicated that even its designer could barely find his way out.

○ **INVENTED HUMAN FLIGHT LONG BEFORE THE WRIGHT BROTHERS** King Minos locked up Daedalus to keep the solution to the Labyrinth from getting out. Using only wax and feathers, Daedalus built two sets of wings that allowed him and his son Icarus to escape from the tower. (Tragically, Icarus flew too close to the sun and the wax on his wings melted away. A fatal mistake!)

○ **THREADED A SEASHELL** King Minos promised a reward to anyone who could pass a thread through the winding insides of a triton seashell. Daedalus thought a moment, then tied the thread to an ant, put the ant in the seashell, and dabbed some honey at the shell's other end. The ant crawled through, threading the shell!

Palamedes

Mental Feats:

○ **INVENTED CONSONANTS** Supposedly the Fates invented the first Greek alphabet, but they stopped after inventing the vowels, plus the equivalents of *B* and *T*. It butt ab beet abt to tabt bat teb! Oops, I mean: It must have been hard to talk back then! Palamedes solved the problem by inventing the other eleven Greek consonants.

○ **INVENTED EVERYTHING ELSE TOO** In various myths: counting, money, dice, military ranks, weights, measures, and jokes.

○ **OUTSMARTED ODYSSEUS!** That's how you know he *really* deserves to be number one. Crafty Odysseus didn't want to go fight at Troy, so he pretended to be crazy, hooking a donkey to his plow and sowing his fields with salt! Palamedes suspected a trick, and placed Odysseus's infant son Telemachus in the path of the plow. Odysseus revealed his sanity by stopping the plow just in time.

SEVENTH PERIOD

Where the Wild Things Were

What good is it to tell stories about mighty gods and brave adventurers if they don't have terrible enemies to menace them? The Greeks knew that heroes needed monsters, and they created a gallery of monsters so memorable that they're still scaring us today.

Spawn Stars

Just like in real life, many of the most hideous beasts in Greek mythology were siblings. They were the brood of two primordial monsters: Typhon and Echidna.

Typhon was the hugest and deadliest monster ever born. His head reached to the heavens, while his two arms stretched all the way to the east and west. He had dragon heads for fingers, serpent coils for legs, vast wings that blocked out the sun, and fire spewing from his eyes and mouth. Gaea raised him up out of Tartarus in revenge after Zeus and the other gods defeated the Titans and the Giants.

Blow by Blow

Even though the Greeks used the word "Typhon" to refer to hot, stormy winds, this probably isn't the source of our word "typhoon," which comes from a Chinese source: *tai fung*, meaning "big wind."

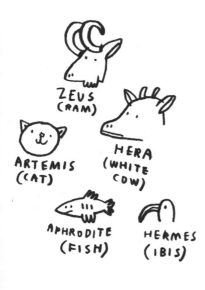

ZEUS
(RAM)

ARTEMIS
(CAT)

HERA
(WHITE
COW)

APHRODITE
(FISH)

HERMES
(IBIS)

Echidna was Typhon's mate: a beautiful woman from the waist up, a great speckled serpent below. She dwelled in the cave of Arima with her ferocious brood of monster babies and ate men raw.

When Typhon stormed the gates of Olympus, even the gods were frightened, and they fled disguised as animals.

Typhon caught Zeus, used his snake coils to snatch away Zeus's sickle (the same one Cronus used on Uranus back on page 25), crippled Zeus with the sickle, and dragged the once-mighty god to his cave!

Hermes and Pan saved the day by following Typhon back to the cave, stealing Zeus's sinews, and sewing them back onto Zeus's arms and legs so the god could move again. A furious Zeus thundered back at Typhon, ripping entire mountains from the earth and hurling them at the monster. Finally, he pinned him beneath Mount Etna, where Typhon continued

spewing fire and lava. Hephaestus placed his forge atop the mountain, an active volcano to this day.

Typhon and Echidna's offspring included some monsters you'll remember from the tales of Heracles: the Nemean lion, the Hydra, the dragon Ladon, and Cerberus. Now let's meet their brothers and sisters!

Riddle Me This

Remember when Oedipus accidentally killed his birth father, Laius, on his way to the city of Thebes (page 115)? Laius was headed to Delphi to ask the oracle what to do about the Sphinx, a monster from the wastes of Ethiopia whom the gods had sent to menace Thebes.

The Sphinx sat on Mount Phicium, outside the city walls, and she asked every passerby the same riddle:

"What creature walks on four legs in the morning, two legs in the afternoon, and three legs in the evening?"

. . . and strangled and devoured them when they didn't know the answer.

When Oedipus reached Thebes, the Sphinx asked him the same riddle. Oedipus thought for a minute, and then replied, "Man. He crawls on all fours as a baby, walks upright in his youth, and leans on a staff in his old age."

The Sphinx screamed horribly and threw herself off the cliff. The people of Thebes acclaimed Oedipus as their new king.

Monster Mash

The Sphinx, the Greeks said, had the head of a woman, the body of a lion, the wings of an eagle, and the tail of a serpent. In fact, this is how the Greeks dreamed up most of their mythical creatures: by mixing and matching body parts from *real* animals, like a hideous, nightmarish version of Build-A-Bear Workshop. Let's take a look, shall we?

man + horse = CENTAUR

man + goat = SATYR

horse + bird = PEGASUS

man + bull = MINOTAUR

woman + bird = HARPY

eagle + lion = GRIFFIN

snake x 100 = HYDRA

horse + fish = HIPPOCAMPUS

horse + rooster = HIPPOALECTRYON

woman + lion + eagle + serpent = SPHINX

lion + goat + dragon = CHIMERA

(dog x 3) + dragon = CERBERUS

woman + (snake x 1,000) + bird + boar = GORGON

Don't Kill the Messenger

The Chimera was a terrible, flame-snorting monstrosity that rampaged all over the land of Lycia. It had the front of a lion, the body of a goat, and the tail of a dragon—and the heads of all three! No one could get close enough to the terrible beast to do battle with it.

Enter Bellerophon! Bellerophon had angered King Proetus of Tiryns, who sent him on to Lycia bearing a sealed note. The note said:

KILL THE MAN WHO BEARS THIS NOTE!

That King Proetus! What a prankster.

Proetus, you see, didn't want to directly murder a guest in his home, since that would anger the Furies. But the king of Lycia didn't want to kill a guest either, for the

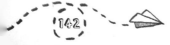

same reason. Instead, he decided to send Bellerophon to fight the Chimera!

On his journey to the Chimera, Bellerophon fell asleep one night in the temple of Athena, who whispered to him that he could kill the beast with the help of Pegasus, and she left him a magical golden bridle to help tame the beautiful winged horse.

Once astride Pegasus, Bellerophon let fly a cascade of arrows from above to weaken the Chimera, but the flames from its three mouths were too hot for him to deliver the final blow. That's when he had a stroke of inspiration: He put a lump of lead on the tip of his spear and lowered it toward the beast's jaws. The Chimera's fiery breath melted the lead, which ran down its throat and cooked it from the inside out.

The Amazing Race

One of Echidna's most unusual children was the Teumessian vixen, a giant fox so swift it could never be caught. Amphitryon's plan was to rid his kingdom of the fox using Laelaps, a hunting dog that could catch any prey. What happens when an inescapable hound chases an uncatchable fox? Zeus got a headache and resolved the paradox by turning both to stone.

Between the Devil and the Deep Blue Sea

The Strait of Messina, between Sicily and Italy, was guarded by two fearful dangers. Scylla had twelve dangling legs, six heads that yelped like dogs, and a triple row of sharp teeth in each mouth.

Across the strait was Charybdis, a demonic whirlpool monster with a giant mouth that flushed like a gigantic toilet three times a day with enough force to drag a ship underwater.

Most monsters in Greek myth get slain by a hero, but Scylla and Charybdis are so powerful that the trick is just to sneak past them. The sorceress Circe told Odysseus how to accomplish this: to sail past at top speed while hugging close to Scylla's side of the channel. Odysseus lost six men as Scylla's six jaws clamped down on them, but the rest of his crew survived.

Hair Trigger

In some myths the Gorgons were the offspring of Typhon and Echidna as well.

There were three of these terrible snake-haired women, with great feathered wings, brass claws, and boars' tusks. Just one lock of their writhing hair was enough to scatter an entire army. Stheno and Euryale were immortal, but their sister, Medusa, could be killed—luckily for the hero Perseus!

Perseus had boasted that he would kill Medusa—to impress a princess, of course. Normally, this would have been a terrible idea, since Medusa could freeze a man to stone with just one glance from her terrifying eyes. But Perseus had the help of the gods in his quest: Athena gave him a brightly polished shield, and Hermes gave him an adamantine sickle. However, he still needed three more things.

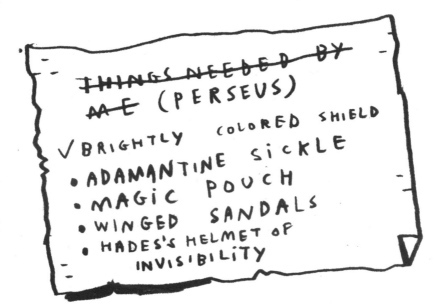

THINGS NEEDED BY
ME (PERSEUS)

✓ BRIGHTLY COLORED SHIELD
• ADAMANTINE SICKLE
• MAGIC POUCH
• WINGED SANDALS
• HADES'S HELMET OF
  INVISIBILITY

Only the Graeae, the blind Gray Sisters, knew where the pouch, the sandals, and the helmet were. Perseus stole their single eye and tooth, refusing to  return them until the sisters told him where he could find the last three things he needed.

Once he collected the items, Perseus used the winged sandals to fly to the Land of the Hyperboreans. Using the helmet of invisibility, he crept up on the Gorgons from behind while they slept, making sure he only looked at them in their reflections on his shield. After he sliced off Medusa's head with his sickle, he placed it in his magic pouch for the journey home.

I Am Woman, Hear Me Boar

No monster took more heroes to kill than the Calydonian Boar, sent by an angry Artemis when the king of Calydon neglected a sacrifice to her. Dozens of brave adventurers banded together to track the giant boar, though some refused to hunt because Atalanta—*a woman!*—had been invited along. It was Meleager's sword that delivered the killing blow, but he declined the prize, correctly noting that Atalanta's arrow had struck the boar first, critically wounding it.

Bull Sessions

ABOMINA-BULL! When the king and queen of the island of Crete refused to sacrifice the beautiful snow-white bull Poseidon had sent them, the sea god grew angry. When the queen next gave birth, her child was the ugliest baby anyone had ever seen. You know that ugly baby you saw that one time? *Much worse.* The creature was half-man and half-bull, and only the taste of human flesh could satisfy its hunger.

IMPENETRA-BULL! King Minos of Crete had Daedalus build an impossibly complicated maze under the palace to imprison the monster called the Minotaur. When the Minotaur was hungry, it would shake the castle with its hungry roars, so Minos demanded that Athens send seven strong young men and seven maidens to be fed to the Minotaur.

The black-sailed ships journeyed to Crete every nine years, full of the sacrificial victims.

INDOMITA-BULL! The Athenian hero Theseus decided enough was enough. The third time the boats were due to sail, he took the place of one of the seven youths. He was so confident that he would defeat the Minotaur that he brought with him a white sail, so that when the boats returned, he could signal his father, King Aegeus, that his mission had been successful.

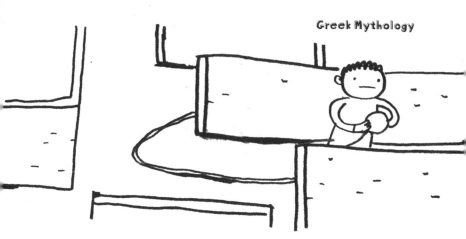

KNOWLEDGEA-BULL! When Theseus arrived in Crete, the king's daughter Ariadne immediately fell in love with him, and said she would help him kill the Minotaur if he would take her back to Athens as his wife. She gave Theseus the secret to the Labyrinth: a magic ball of thread invented by Daedalus that would unroll to the heart of the maze and then let the user find his way back to the entrance. Theseus made his way to the Minotaur's lair that night, seized the horrible thing by its hair, and sacrificed it to Poseidon with a sword.

REGRETTA-BULL! But the happy couple didn't even last the voyage home. The god Dionysus spied the beautiful Ariadne and wanted her to be his bride, so he ordered Theseus to leave her sleeping on the island of Naxos. Theseus was so bummed returning to Athens without his love that he forgot to put up the white sails. When King Aegeus saw the black-sailed ship returning home, he assumed Theseus was dead and threw himself into the sea in grief. It's still called the Aegean Sea today.

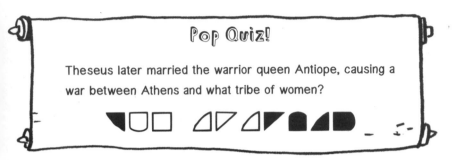

Pop Quiz!

Theseus later married the warrior queen Antiope, causing a war between Athens and what tribe of women?

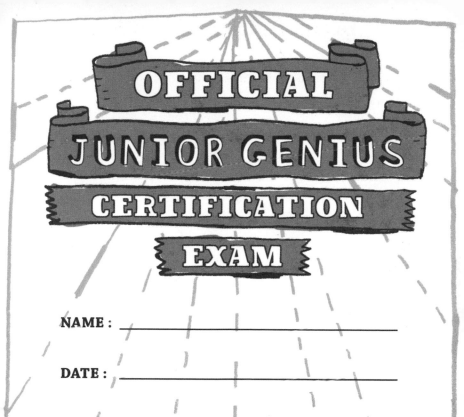

OFFICIAL JUNIOR GENIUS CERTIFICATION EXAM

NAME : _____

DATE : _____

We've stuffed a lot of facts in your brains today, class. Will they emerge fully grown when you need them, like Athena from the skull of Zeus? It's time to see if you're ready to officially certify as a Junior Genius in Greek Mythology. Sharpen your number two pencils and turn the page when I say "Begin."

Wait for it.

Wait for it . . .

BEGIN.

OFFICIAL JUNIOR GENIUS CERTIFICATION EXAM

1. The gods of Olympus had ichor instead of what?

(A) Wine

(B) Blood

(C) Anger

(D) Chess

2. What was left in Pandora's jar when she closed the lid?

(A) Pain

(B) Hope

(C) Fear

(D) Those Styrofoam packing peanuts

3. Which of these foes from Heracles's labors had just one head?

(A) The Nemean lion

(B) Geryon

(C) The Hydra

(D) Cerberus

4. What was wrong with the prophecies of poor Cassandra?

(A) They were all wrong.

(B) They came too late.

(C) No one believed them.

(D) They were riddles.

5. Where was the oracle to Apollo that the Greeks believed was the center of the world?

(A) Didyma

(B) Dodona

(C) Corinth

(D) Delphi

6. What sorceress showed Jason how to retrieve the Golden Fleece?

   Ⓐ Circe   Ⓑ Ariadne

   Ⓒ Medea   Ⓓ Andromeda

7. Niobe foolishly boasted to the gods about the size of her what?

   Ⓐ Family   Ⓑ Kingdom

   Ⓒ Crown   Ⓓ Nose

8. The city of Athens is named for Athena because she gave it what valuable gift?

   Ⓐ The chariot   Ⓑ The loom

   Ⓒ The ram   Ⓓ The olive

9. Daedalus built the Labyrinth to imprison what creature?

   Ⓐ The Minotaur   Ⓑ The Chimera

   Ⓒ The Sphinx   Ⓓ A Harpy

10. What king foolishly judged Pan a better musician than Apollo?

   Ⓐ Sisyphus   Ⓑ Midas

   Ⓒ Admetus   Ⓓ Peleus

11. Which of these groups of mythical sisters was not a trio?

Ⓐ The Graces   Ⓑ The Fates

Ⓒ The Hours   Ⓓ The Muses

12. Which goddess was born when she arose from the sea foam off Cyprus one morning?

Ⓐ Aphrodite   Ⓑ Artemis

Ⓒ Athena   Ⓓ Demeter

13. What was Charon's job in Greek mythology?

Ⓐ Ferrying souls to Hades   Ⓑ Tutoring heroes

Ⓒ Guarding the gates of Olympus   Ⓓ Driving the sun chariot

14. What profession claimed Hephaestus as its patron god?

Ⓐ Sailors   Ⓑ Farmers

Ⓒ Blacksmiths   Ⓓ Thieves

15. With whom did Echo fall in love after losing her power of speech?

Ⓐ Hyacinth   Ⓑ Leander

Ⓒ Narcissus   Ⓓ Tantalus

16. Where do the gods Nereus, Triton, Proteus, and Glaucus live?

    Ⓐ The underworld   Ⓑ Mount Olympus

    Ⓒ The forest   Ⓓ The sea

17. Who invented the wooden horse that ended the Trojan War?

    Ⓐ Agamemnon   Ⓑ Achilles

    Ⓒ Hector   Ⓓ Odysseus

18. Which of these Greek gods had no Roman equivalent?

    Ⓐ Ares   Ⓑ Hades

    Ⓒ Apollo   Ⓓ Poseidon

19. Achilles was almost invulnerable because his mother had dipped him in what?

    Ⓐ Fire   Ⓑ The River Styx

    Ⓒ Nectar   Ⓓ Centaur's blood

20. What did Cronus swallow, thinking it was his youngest son, Zeus?

    Ⓐ A pig   Ⓑ A rock

    Ⓒ A bronze anvil   Ⓓ A melon

All right, pencils down! Turn the page to
the answers and see how you did.

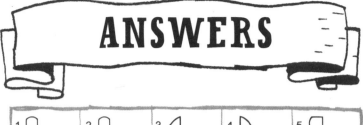

ANSWERS

1. ◯	2. ◯	3. ◸	4. ◺	5. ◯
6. ◺	7. ◸	8. ◯	9. ◸	10. ◯
11. ◯	12. ◸	13. ◸	14. ◺	15. ◺
16. ◯	17. ◯	18. ◺	19. ◯	20. ◯

Scoring

16–20	Certified Junior Genius!
13–15	Almost Olympian
10–12	Nothing to Apollo-gize For
6–9	The Minus Touch
0–5	Lost in the Labyrinth

Did you make the cut, Junior Genius? Well done! You can print out your official certificate at JuniorGeniusGuides.com.

If not, don't worry—*you can still pass!* Go ahead and review the course material, and when you're feeling as clever as Daedalus, take another shot. Repeat until you know your mythology backward and forward, or have at least memorized the pattern of answer letters. Anyone who likes learning stuff can be a Junior Genius . . . eventually!

HOMEWORK

We only scratched the surface of Greek mythology today, Junior Geniuses. There are hundreds of great stories we didn't have time to tell, and I hope you look for them in your local library. Here are some other ways to dig into the world of ancient Greece without becoming an archaeologist and flying to the Mediterranean.

○ **Unleash the power of Atlas** Lots of the regions, cities, and bodies of water mentioned in Greek myth can still be found on a modern map of Greece. Buy or draw your own mythology map for your wall, and use pins to mark where different stories took place.

○ **Give birth to a brood of monsters** The Greeks invented their mythical monsters by combining the powers of real-life animals. Why not do the same? Ask friends or family to suggest a few animals, then draw and name a combined version. Would the Argonauts themselves be able to defeat your monkey-rhino-squid hybrid? Maybe not, if you gave it enough tentacles.

○ **Become a word detective** We've already seen lots of English words that come from Greek myths: "music," "panic," "echo." Here are a few more with mythological roots you can investigate.

calypso	jovial	paean
cereal	lethargic	psyche
halcyon	mentor	tantalize
hermetic	nemesis	stentorian

○ **Spot the mistakes** Now that you're an expert on Greek myths, try reading or watching a *modern* story that borrows mythological themes: Rick Riordan's *Percy Jackson* books, the *Clash of the Titans* movies, Disney's *Hercules*, or even *Wonder Woman* comics. What parts of the original myths did the writers get right? Which things did they change?

THE FINAL BELL

Would you believe there was an American president who . . .

○ Was so ambidextrous that he could write in Greek with his left hand and Latin with his right—at the same time?

○ Gave a seemingly endless two-hour speech at his own inauguration, outdoors on a cold wet day, and then died of pneumonia just a month later?

○ Once lost an entire box of priceless White House china by betting it in a poker game?

We'll meet these three chief executives and forty-one others in our next class, when we time-travel more than three thousand years forward from ancient Greece to learn about more recent history. I'll see you again in **Ken Jennings' Junior Genius Guides: U.S. Presidents.**

Before we go, let's stand and quote the great French scientist Blaise Pascal as we recite the official Junior Genius Slogan:

"It is much better to know something about everything than everything about something."

Class dismissed!